PAWPRINTS ON OUR SOULS

A Recent Associated Press poll found that for the first time, two-thirds of Americans agree with the basic tenet of the animal welfare movement: "An animal's right to live free of suffering should be just as important as a person's right to live free of suffering."

"Things have changed," said Ingrid Newkird, co-founder of PETA(People for the Ethical Treatment of Animals). "Even in steak houses, you find vegetarian items."

PAWPRINTS is an easy to read short book laced with brief facts, dotted with supporting quotes by celebrities and doctors. This book was designed to be read in any order. Feel free to open any page and scan paragraphs and quotes of interest.

Foley Publishing Company supports the animal welfare movement in accordance with Gandhi's view: "I do not believe in short-violent cuts to success... However much I may sympathize with and admire worthy motives, I am an uncompromising opponent of violent methods even to serve the noblest causes... Experience teaches me that permanent good can never be the outcome of.... violence."

Gandhi

PAWPRINTS ON OUR SOULS

(Nothing Wrong Comes Out Right)

by

S. Francis

Foley Publishing Company

A Foley Publishing Paperback
PAWPRINTS ON OUR SOULS
This edition published 1999
By Foley Publishing Company
PO Box 32
Port Costa, Ca 94569
All Rights Reserved

ISBN: 0-9667174-0-6

Printed in the USA by

MORRIS PUBLISHING

3212 East Highway 30 • Kearney, NE 68847 • 1-800-650-7888

Dedication & Acknowledgments

This book is dedicated to the memory of Linda McCartney(1941-1998), a staunch anti-vivisectionist, vegetarian, and long-time supporter of animal welfare organizations such as PETA, which operates under the simple principle: Animals are not ours to eat, wear, experiment on, or use for entertainment.

Linda and her husband Paul were instrumental working with PETA in successful campaigns to stop General Motors' crash tests using animals, Gillette's product tests on animals, and helped ban fur prizes on "Wheel of Fortune."

The McCartneys also edited a graphic-video to show the public the actual cruelty behind the scenes in the fur trade, meat trade, and animal testing laboratories.

In 1997, Linda, ailing with cancer, helped Paul and PETA rescue 126 Beagles from a U.K. animal breeder, who planned to sell them to a laboratory where they would be poisoned.

Linda also published several cookbooks and marketed her own line of meatless meals. She even shipped tons of her vegetarian food to feed starving children in Bosnia.

I would also like to thank Janet-Kuhlmann Foley, my supportive wife, an accomplished artist, and always an amicable copyeditor.

A special thanks to PETA, Animal Rights Online, American Anti-Vivisection Society, Association of Veterinarians for Animal Rights(AVAR), EnviroLink, In Defense of Animals, The Humane Society, and other animal welfare organizations for their permission to use certain materials such as Doctors Quotes, some of which are from "1000 Doctors(and more)Against Vivisection" by Hans Reusch.

Reflections

"No one is *GOOD* but only God."

Jesus Christ
Mark 10

As for vivisectors, factory farmers, and other animal exploiters, "Nobody ever does anything deliberately in the interests of evil, for the sake of evil. Everybody acts in the interests of good, as he understands it. But everybody understands it in a different way. Consequently men drown, slay, and kill one another in the interests of good."

Gurdjieff
Esoteric Teacher

"The individual is capable of both great compassion and great indifference. He has it within his means to nourish the former and outgrow the latter."

Norman Cousins
Philosopher & Author

"Cowardice asks the question, 'Is it safe?'
Expediency asks the question, 'Is it polite?'
Vanity asks the question, 'Is it popular?'
But Conscience asks the question, 'Is it right?'
And there comes a point when one must take a position that is neither safe, nor polite, nor popular, but he must take it because his conscience tells him that it is right..."

Martin Luther King, Jr.

Contents

TAX DOLLARS FOR PAIN

"I am in favor of animal rights as well as human rights. That is the way of a whole human being."

Abraham Lincoln

"The AIDS virus, which is believed by many to have come from(experiments on?) African monkeys... 'The animals don't get sick, so we didn't know it existed,' said Jonathan Allan of the Southwest Foundation in San Antonio, which studies primates,'" in response to the danger of transplanting animal organs to humans, a money-making-machine for vivisectors at many leading universities, research institutes, and biotechnology firms.

Knight-Ridder Newspapers

The United States National Institute of Health(NIH), is documented to be the world's largest financier of animal research, doling out *MILLIONS* each year in tax-dollar-grants for animal experiments.

"Until we stop harming all other living beings, we are still savages. Non-violence leads to the highest ethics, which is the goal of all evolution."   Thomas Edison

VIVISECTION means cutting into, dissecting, or experimenting on living animals. The practice reportedly got its start because of religious prohibitions against dissecting human cadavers. When the religious stigma faded, vivisection had become entrenched in the medical and educational institutions, feeding off tax dollars in the form of grant money. Countless case studies confirm, that vivisection research uses and exploits animals, then discards them like disposable tools.

Medical research often *intentionally* causes pain, *unnecessarily* on *un-consenting* healthy animals.

"I abhor vivisection. It should at least be curbed. Better, it should be abolished. I know of no achievement through vivisection, no scientific discovery, that could not have been obtained without such barbarism and cruelty. The whole thing is evil."

Dr. Charles Mayo
World Renowned Mayo Clinic

According to the Animal Welfare Movement, an assemblage of animal welfare groups including the Society for the Prevention of Cruelty to Animals and the Humane Society, each year approximately 200 million animals worldwide are exploited in experiments, such as deliberately crippling, burning, electrocuting, wounding and mutilating animals in the name of Frankenstein science for so-called human advances.

Every year in just the U.S., nearly 100 million animals are killed with your tax dollars in federally-funded universities, hospitals, commercial and military laboratories.

"Atrocities are not less atrocities when they occur in laboratories and are called medical research."

George Bernard Shaw
Nobel Prize Playwright

The TV show Dateline, reported that 101,000 dogs were

sacrificed in U.S. animal experiments in just one year. Many came from dog-nappers who answered *Free To Good Home* newspaper ads then sold the dogs for $55. to $500. to hospitals and medical centers such as LA's Cedars-Sinai, and other prominent universities and veteran research administrations performing animal experiments, that routinely purchase the dogs from notorious breeders known as butchers.

"Many vivisectors still claim that what they do helps save human lives. They are lying. The truth is that animal experiments kill people, and animal researchers are responsible for the deaths of thousands of men, women, and children every year."

Dr. Vernon Coleman
Fellow of the Royal Society of Medicine, UK

"Polio could be dealt with only by preventing the irreversible destruction of the large number of motor nerve cells, and the work on prevention was delayed by an erroneous conception of the nature of the human disease based on misleading models of the disease in monkeys."

Dr. Albert Sabin, Developer of Oral Polio Vaccine
Congressional Testimony on Dangers of Animal-based Research

The Physicians Committee For Responsible Medicine, states that animals are different anatomically, genetically, immunologically, and physiologically from each other and humans, so they react differently to different substances. Drugs that are safe to certain animals are carcinogenic to humans and vice-versa. Even human diseases artificially induced in animals, often manifest themselves differently.

"The discovery of chemotherapeutic agents for the treatment of human cancer is widely heralded as a triumph due to use of animal model systems. However, here again, these exaggerated claims are coming from or are endorsed by the same people who get the federal dollars for animal research. There is little, if any, factual evidence

9

that would support these claims.

Indeed while conflicting animal results have often delayed and hampered advances in the war on cancer, they have never produced a single substantial advance in the prevention or treatment of human cancer."

Dr. Irwin Bross
Congressional Testimony

As reported on Paul Harvey's radio commentary, despite the government's own studies that high tech, mechanical, and human tissue and cells' testing methods are much more accurate than animal testing, the government continues animal testing and still mandates animal experiments before pharmaceuticals can be marketed (Paul Harvey sighed disgustedly). According to the U.S. General Accounting Office, 198 new drugs passed animal testing during an eleven year period, but 102 of these drugs proved to be toxic to humans.

The drugs Thalidomide, Opren, Clioquinol and Zomax passed animal testing but had disastrous effects on the humans who used them.

Thalidomide was estimated to cause 10,000 worldwide birth defects. Clioquinol caused 30,000 cases of blindness and paralysis, and is blamed for thousands of deaths.

Opren killed 70 people and caused serious side effects, such as kidney, liver, eye damage to an estimated 3,500.

Zomax, a common painkiller killed 14 people and had life-threatening allergic reactions in hundreds of other people before it was withdrawn.

"I am not interested to know whether vivisection produces results that are profitable to the human race or doesn't...The pain which it inflicts upon unconsenting animals is the basis of my enmity toward it, and it is to me sufficient justification of the enmity without looking further."

Mark Twain

According to the Manual of Animal Rights, along with the financial interests of medical researchers, pharmaceutical companies, animal breeders, surgical instruments and cage and restraining devices manufacturers and distributors... the entire livelihoods of many researchers are rooted in animal experiments. Even the former chair of the Pro-Vivisection, Research Defense Society admitted: "The real motives(for animal research) are a mixture in varying proportions of scientific curiosity, desire to explore new fields, desire for recognition and fame, and career ambition..."

"The pressure on young doctors to publish and the availability of laboratory animals have made professional advancement the main reason for animal experiments."

Dr. E. J.H. Moore
VP of Doctors in Britain Against Animal Experiments

The largest animal breeding company for laboratory testing in the United States is reported to be Charles River Breeding Laboratories(CRBL) in Massachusetts, owned by Bausch and Lomb.

"Results from animal tests are not transferable between species, and therefore cannot guarantee product safety for humans...In reality these tests do not provide protection for consumers from unsafe products, but rather they are used to protect corporations from legal liability."

Dr. Herbert Gundersheimer
Physicians Committee For Responsible Medicine

According to the Associated Press, the all-powerful American Medical Association(AMA) was the top lobby spender, smoothing Washington politicians with over $8.5 million in a six month period, to ensure their key financial interests of maintaining the status quo for their pet-projects, such as huge government grants for animal research and blocking Universal Healthcare (the insurance companies are also committed to blocking Universal Healthcare) for Americans, which despite their propaganda, is apparently successful in other countries and even in Hawaii.

"I care not much for a man's religion whose dog and cat are not the better for it."

Abraham Lincoln

The Animal Welfare Act passed in 1966 and amended in 1970, 1976, 1985, set standards for animal housing, handling, feeding and transporting experimental animals, but because of the economic pressure from vivisectors placed no restrictions on the experimental conditions, in essence a paper-tiger: "Nothing in these rules, regulations, or standards shall effect or interfere with the design, outline, or performance of actual research or experimentation by a research facility as determined by such research facility." Compliance is at the direction of the research institution, and doesn't protect mice, rats, birds or farm animals.

"There are, in fact, only two categories of doctors and scientists who are not opposed to vivisection: those who don't know enough about it, and those who make money from it."

Dr. Werner Hartinger
President of League of German Doctors Against Vivisection

Cancer and heart disease are still the two leading causes of death, despite a century of millions of cruel experiments on animals, in the $-business-$ of looking for a cure for cancer and heart disease.

"The abolition of vivisection would in no way halt medical progress, just the opposite is the case. All the sound medical knowledge of today stems from observations carried out on human beings. No surgeon can gain least knowledge from experiments on animals, and all the great surgeons of the past and of the present day are in agreement on that."

Dr. Bruno Fedi, Director of the Institute of Pathological Anatomy
General Hospital,Terni, Italy

Even statistically speaking, vivisection is a failure. Since 1950, 144,000,000 animals have been killed in British animal research labs, yet the life expectancy for the middle-aged in Britain has not increased since this date.

"The bold new theory of Dr. Irwin Bross holds that most cancer and heart disease is actually caused by environmental damage of human DNA. The theory cannot be proven in animal experiments, and so it is steadfastly resisted by the biomedical establishment."

Dr. Brandon Reines

"It was not medical research that stamped out tuberculosis, diphtheria, pneumonia and puerperal sepsis; the primary credit for those monumental accomplishments must go to public health, sanitation and the general improvement in the standard of living brought about by industrialization."

Dr. Edward Kass
Harvard Medical School

The American Cancer Society, American Heart Association, March of Dimes, Red Cross, etc. continue to solicit your money to conduct gruesome and useless experiments on millions of animals (see Hell Holes), even though the Knight Ridder Newspapers reported the first slight drop in cancer deaths in 100 years(.05%) was from lifestyle changes: less smokers, reduced

13

workplace toxins, early detection, etc., not the $35 billion spent on animal experiments just in the U.S. since 1975: such as severing nerves, slicing throats, and sewing eyes shut..., sometimes even without any anesthesia on dogs, kittens, monkeys, etc.

"Another basic problem which we share as a result of the regulations and the things that prompted them is unscientific pre-occupation with animal studies. Animal studies are done for legal reasons and not for scientific reasons. The predictive value of such studies for man is often meaningless—which means our research may be meaningless.

Dr. James G. Gallagher Former
Director of Medical Research Lederle Laboratories

The Physicians Committee For Responsible Medicine (PCFRM), states that most life threatening diseases like heart disease, could be avoided if people would maintain vegetarian diets, exercise, and not abuse alcohol and smoking. The PCFRM claims these simple changes would also help prevent arthritis, adult-onset diabetes, ulcers and many other illnesses.

"As a researcher I am involved with mutagenesis and cancerogenesis, two areas in which experimentation is fundamentally indispensable. I therefore know what I am talking about. And I say NO to vivisection. Not only on ethical, but above all on scientific grounds. It has been proved that the results of research with animals are in no case valid for man.

There is a law of Nature in relation to metabolism, according to which a biochemical reaction that one has established in one species only applies to that species, and not to any other. Two closely related species, like the mouse and the rat, often react entirely differently..."

Gianni Tamino,
Researcher University of Padua, Italy's Premier Medical University

14

According to the Manual of Animal Rights, because of experiments on animals blood transfusions were delayed 200 years by misleading and wrong information from vivisection. Corneal transplants were delayed 90 years. Many advances in medicine, such as insulin, were developed in spite of rather than thanks to animal research.

"Animal models differ from their human counterparts. Conclusions drawn from animal research, when applied to human disease, are likely to delay progress, mislead and do harm to the patient."
Dr. Moneim A. Fadali, Cardiac/Thoracic Surge
UCLA Faculty Board of Directors

Vivisection is the cruel science of the past states the Manual For Animal Rights. To insure their livelihoods, vivisectors often mislead the public with fear: Wouldn't you rather see animals experimented on to save sick children? Gratefully, the decision is not between experimenting on animals or saving sick loved ones. Thousands of children and others continue to lose their lives because of the deceptive results and precious time wasted from vivisection, rather than concentrating on the promising new techniques, such as: genetic engineering and growing human cells that offer life rather than cruelty.

"Like everyone else in my profession, I use to be of the opinion that we owe nearly all our knowledge of medical and surgical science to animal experiments. Today I know that precisely the opposite is the case. In surgery especially, they(operating on animals to learn) are of no help to the practitioner, indeed he is often led astray by them."
Dr. Bigelow
Former Vivisector

Vivisectors falsely clamor that the horrible abuses of the recent past such as the Navy Sea Dog experiments documented in Ingrid Newkirks's(Co-Founder of PETA) book, *Free The Animals*,

15

have stopped. From 1937 onward, 2-to-100 dogs at a time were exploited in redundant decompression experiments. One of the common experiments was to put dogs into stereotaxic devices, and peel their skin and muscles back over their noses and skulls to insert electrodes into their heads, then submerge the dogs into deep tanks to simulate diving...then kill the dogs after the experiment. To the Navy's credit, former enlisted personnel tipped off the Animal Liberation Front.

"He who won't hesitate to vivisect, won't hesitate to lie about it."

George Bernard Shaw

Another redundant Navy decompression experiment was to place un-anesthetized dogs into airtight boxes vented with pure oxygen ...until they died...any dogs still alive 90-hours later were killed. These and other painful decompression experiments began as early as 1854, despite the Navy's own documentation: "Be advised, findings in dogs cannot be extrapolated to man."

The Navy's files also contained drowning experiments on cats, rats, monkeys, and dogs, the Navy contracted with leading universities for over 40-years.

"In their behavior toward creatures, all men all Nazis."

Isaac Bashevis Singer
Author

The vivisectors and their supporters continued ranting in the 1990s, that the harrowing abuses of yesterday had stopped, but surprise inspections to several research facilities and hospitals by PETA and tips from enlightened insiders proved otherwise.

"My doctrine is this, that if we see cruelty or wrong that we have the power to stop, and do nothing, we make ourselves sharers in the guilt."

Anna Sewell
Author

Records from the prestigious City of Hope, a federally founded animal research facility, that also elicited lots of money from unsuspecting movie stars, supported PETA's finding that animals were left un-attended for up to 20-hours. And only 23 of the 54 dogs scheduled for cancer experiments survived till the actual experiment. The causes of death were infections, poisoning, anesthesia overdoses, gross negligence and deplorable living conditions.

"Life is life—whether in a cat, or dog or man(who had a choice). There is no difference there between a cat or a man. The idea of difference is a human conception for man's own advantage..."
Sir Aurobindo
Poet and Philosopher

The City of Hope had also been cited in the 1980s for cruelty to dogs and cats, also depicted in the book *Free The Animals*. According to inside-tipsters, experimental (unnecessary) surgery was being performed without anesthesia and the animals were left to die on cement floors in their own filth, behind the impressive medical buildings.

Many dead puppies and bleeding animals were scattered throughout the facility. Photographs backed-up the charges and much more. Most of these dogs were beagles bred to be experimented on, which researchers rationalize makes-it-moral to use and abuse these frightened and tortured animals that never had a chance from birth.

"It were much better that a sentient being should never have existed, than that it should have existed only to endure unmitigated misery."
Percy Bysshe Shelley
Poet

Inspections by Peta throughout the 1990s also found gross neglect in the scabies laboratories at Wright State University(WSU).

The veterinarian in charge would not allow treatment to suffering animals. The dogs and rabbits died alone after suffering for days or weeks. Even the NIH cited them for 10 pages of violations, such as bludgeoning animals to death with a claw hammer then eating them.

To desensitize the experimenters, the vivisectors were encouraged to deride the tormented animals. One distressed dog at WSU who circled perpetually in her cage was called Dizzy, till her death after many experiments.

"Mutilating animals and calling it science condemns the human species to moral and intellectual hell...this hideous Dark Age of the mindless torture of animals must be overcome."

Grace Slick
Musician

Again at WSU, one dog died after experiments and was cut open and autopsied while a living dog watched his waiting fate. By blowing the whistle, three employees put their careers on the line.

"Vivisection is the blackest of all the black crimes that a man is at present committing against God and his fair creation."

Ghandi

A baby monkey had her name *CRAP* painfully tattooed onto her forehead at the Royal College of Surgeons.

"My own conviction is that the study of human physiology by way of experiments on animals is the most grotesque and fantastic error ever committed in the whole range of human intellectual activity."

Dr. G.F.Walker

In several primate facilities PETA continues to find abuses such as: monkeys restrained in stereotaxic chairs for days, so the experimenters can conveniently draw blood, ironically conducting AIDS experiments on the very animals AIDS is theorized to originate from during previous vivisection experiments...

18

"Normally, animal experiments not only fail to contribute to the safety of medications, but they even have the opposite effect."

Professor Dr. Kurt Fickentscher
Pharmacological Institute of University of Bonn, Germany

For decades in SEMA, a federally funded laboratory, baby monkeys were taken from their mothers and containerized for years in isolation chambers for redundant deprivation experiments. The babies were hooked up to head electrodes to measure brain activity, and foot shocks were administered for misbehaviors. Often the cramped quarters didn't allow room for the monkeys to move their limbs.

Intermittently they were tormented with natural enemies like snakes and electric shocks so vivisectors could record their mental breakdowns. The monkeys would rock themselves incessantly, mutilate themselves, and eventually die.

"All nature protests against the barbarity of man, who misapprehends, who humiliates, who tortures his inferior brethren."

Jules Michelet, Historian

At the University of Pennsylvania PETA caught researchers pounding baboons senseless with repeated head-blows, then taunting the incapacitated animals. They were cited for 74 documented incidents of animal abuse.

"All that is necessary for the triumph of evil is for good men to do nothing."

Edmund Burke
Statesman and Author

Healthy monkeys' spines have been crushed in vain for over 15-years in medical research experiments studying human paralyses.

19

"Animal tests conducted to establish the effect of medicaments for humans are nonsense."

Professor Dr. Hardegg
Former Vivisector

Despite what vivisectors and their supporters claim, there are still Hitler-vivisectors like Dr. Barbara Gordon-Lickey at the University of Oregon, who for decades sewed kittens' eyes shut and forced them to jump from a tower, so she could study sight deprivation.

These sadistic researchers receive prestigious honors and accolades from the powers-who-be in sanitized news reports to garner more grant money, never mentioning the horrors of animal research, so the public never hears the shrieks of pain and never sees the little terrorized faces and mutilated bodies of this celebrated researcher's handiwork. Many Medical Press Releases are announced as *news* of some great discovery, but usually end with the grant-money-tag: *More studies($$$$) are needed...*

"Every pain I deliberately caused other living beings, I had to endure when I died. In my life review, I realized anybody who deliberately caused animals pain, as soon as they died would have to experience how those animals felt."

Dannion Brinkley
Saved By The Light

Dr. Josef Rauschecker at NIH, implanted electrodes into cats' heads making them endure agonizing *mental health recording sessions* for up two days. Countless cats died painful deaths from white-noise and other abuses, while others simply went mad, till fellow co-workers finally turned him in.

"Bullies are always cowards."

FDR

PETA also found many licensed USDA Class B Dealers with

atrocious histories of animal cruelty, such as leaving dogs tethered to barrels in the sun with no water, dead dogs cramped with live dogs, walking-skeleton-dogs mixed with sick-untreated dogs scattered throughout shanty kennels...but these same kennels were still selling dogs to highly respected research facilities across the country.

"There are endless possibilities for producing irrefutable evidence in support of any theory, through the use of various animal species."
Professor Pietro Croce
Vivisection of Science

PETA routinely finds the procurement forms for several USDA licensed animal dealers, for cruelty devices such as: decapitators, restraining chairs, shock devices, squeeze cages, rat-blenders etc.

"Practically all animal experiments are untenable on a statistical scientific basis, for they possess no scientific validity or reliability. They merely perform an alibi function for pharmaceutical companies, who hope to protect themselves thereby."
Dr. Herbert and Dr. Margot Stiller

At Silver Spring, a Maryland laboratory for behavioral research, police, who are use to grisly crime scenes, were appalled at the cruelty and zero sensitivity of the vivisectors: such as finding a monkey's chopped-off hand being used as a paper weight in an office.

Silver Spring was so deplorable it was the first facility ever raided by the police: monkeys were surgically crippled and left in their stench with no food or water, and many young monkeys who were surgically crippled bit off their fingers, documented once again in the book *Free The Animals*.

Each year in the U.S., an estimated 100 million animals are blinded, maimed, scalded, forced-fed, eardrums punctured, and intentionally hurt in other ways in the name of advancing science by the household products and cosmetic industries, universities, private research facilities, government agencies, and scientific facilities; always ensuring us that animal testing is necessary, and the animals are treated humanely.

"During my medical education at the University of Basle I found vivisection horrible, barbarous, and above all unnecessary."
Carl Jung

Even though the Food and Drug Administration (FDA)doesn't require personal care products, cosmetics, and household products to be tested on animals, many companies still test their products on animals to protect themselves in lawsuits, so they can claim they did everything possible to ensure their products were safe; like employing the dreaded and redundant Draize eye irritancy tests, in which restrained rabbits (rabbits do not have tear ducts), have chemicals sprayed into their eyes and left there to burn, corrode, ulcerate...many of these gently animals go blind in sheer agony.

"I despise and abhor the pleas on behalf of that infamous practice, vivisection. I would rather submit to the worst of deaths, so far as pain goes, than have a single dog or cat tortured on the PRETENSE of sparing me a twinge or two."
Robert Browning
Poet

Today, chemicals are still being routinely pumped into animals' stomachs, massaged into animals' shaved heads and abraded skin. And animals such as dogs, monkeys, rabbits, and rats... are still secluded in chambers and forced to breathe aerosols in quantities that gag them sick or kill them.

"It is well-known that animal effects are often totally different from the effects in people. This applies to substances in medical use as well as substances such as 245 and dioxin."
Dr. Cowan
Medical Officer of Health, New Plymouth, New Zealand

The U.S. Department of Defense spends hundreds of millions of your tax dollars each year, inflicting a half-million healthy animals with wounds, broken bones, blowing out eardrums, burying them alive, blowing them up to measure the blast, radiating them, saturating them with chemical warfare...and other torturous, maiming, and deadly experiments in the name of protecting us. Surely we can be kinder...

"For as long as men massacre animals, they will kill each other. Indeed, he who sows the seed of murder and pain cannot reap joy and love."

Pythagoras
Mathematician

Thousands of doctors now believe vivisection is just cruel and bad science that delays finding a cure and often gives wrong results.

One of countless examples is penicillin. British bacteriologist Alexander Fleming discovered it by accident in 1928. When he returned to his lab after a vacation, he was discarding used culture plates and noticed a mysterious mold had destroyed the disease producing staphylococci bacteria on the plates. Because this mold was a member of the fungus family Penicillium, he called it penicillin.

Fleming tested penicillin on rabbits who had no reaction, because rabbits secrete penicillin, so he gave up.

Two other scientists followed up his work but by luck experimented with mice, merely because of their small size, and stated: "If we had used guinea pigs exclusively we should have said that the penicillin was toxic."

"In the opinion of leading bio-statisticians, it is not possible to transfer the probability predictions from animals to humans...At present, therefore, there exists no possibility at all of scientifically-based prediction.

In this respect, the situation is even less favorable than in game of chance...

In our present state of knowledge, one cannot scientifically determine the probable effect, effectiveness or safety of medicaments when administered to human beings by means of animal experiments...

The example of Thalidomide disaster...illustrates this problem particularly clearly.

Such a medicine-caused disaster could no more be prevented with adequate certainty through animal experimentation today than it could at that time."

Dr. Herbert Hensel
Director of the Institute of Physiology At Marburg University

The link between cigarette smoking and cancer was delayed for decades because of animal experiments. Dogs, monkeys, cats, and rats were subjected to suffocating smoking chambers. The animals got very sick and some died but not from cancer.

In other experiments, monkeys' heads were clamped into helmets so they could hang suspended in midair from spinning carousels, as canons blasted smoke into their faces for hours at a stretch. Some poor monkeys endured this experiment for many years till they got deathly ill and fortunately died, but the monkeys never developed lung cancer, hence doctors even became spokesmen and advertised various smoking brands for extra money.

"There have been many such experiments here and abroad, and none have been able to produce carcinoma of the lung in animals," said Clarence C. Little in the 1961 New England Journal of Medicine.

Only by human studies, called epidemiological studies, did the truth about tobacco come out. But researchers like the easy, laboratory methods that often produce erroneous results rather than the tedious epidemiological studies on the actual human-animal. And millions of dollars of your tax money is specifically slated for research, that is animal research: VIVISECTION.

The following is a glimpse of the insanity of testing drugs on animals:

Aspirin is toxic or causes birth defects in rats, mice, monkeys, guinea pigs, cats and dogs, but is safe for humans.

Aminopterin causes birth defects in humans but is safe for monkeys.

Azathioprine causes birth defects in rabbits but not rats.

Caffeine causes birth defects in rats and mice but not rabbits.

Cortisone causes birth defects in mice and rabbits but no rats.

Thalidomide causes birth defects in humans but not rats and mice.

Nightshade is safe for rabbits but its poisonous leaves are deadly to humans.

"The results of drug experiments upon animals are, as far as their application to man is concerned, absolutely useless and even misleading."

Dr. W. Mitchell Stevens

Many humans would gladly volunteer for medical research, but government regulations forbid it. Government regulations are also to blame for millions of animals sacrificed for unnecessary drug testing.

"Vivisection and sex murder stand on one and the same level, they are the product of spiritual blindness and moral depravity...The alleged objective of working for the good of mankind is a lie. I know that most vivisectors are seeking more to satisfy their vanity than their scientific curiosity. Each of them hopes somehow to make some discovery which, even if it's worthless, is nevertheless a discovery with which one can boast before everyone and throw sand into the eyes of the stupid.

Dr. Franz Harmann

This bizarre and self-serving sadistic theory that animals can't feel pain, was reportedly started by Rene Descartes, a mathematician. And so-called intelligent doctors and researchers believed him, or used it as a wall of defense wanting to believe that animals don't feel pain, no matter what their ears heard and their eyes saw in order to continue their experiments.

"Never believe that animals suffer less than humans. Pain is the same for them that it is for us. Even worse, because they cannot help themselves." Dr. Louis J. Camuti

As ludicrous as it may seem to anyone with common sense at this point in time, but documented in *Free The Animals* and in several published reports, doctors use to subject Afro-Americans to practice-surgeries, stating that black people couldn't feel pain, as with the animals, the cries were just reflex actions.

"I have always felt that the cause of science cannot possibly be served by cruelty to animals, and especially by the barbarous practice of vivisection."

Dr. Robert Howell Perks

Just from 1975 to 1982, vivisectors annihilated more than 38,000 innocent animals to agonizing deaths with radiation, in the $-business-$ of looking for a cure for cancer.

"An infallible characteristic of meanness is cruelty. Men who have practiced tortures on animals without pity, relating them without shame, how can they still hold their heads among human beings?"

Samuel Johnson

Follow the money. In 1996, the Cancer Society, ardent vivisectors, awarded the Mayor of San Francisco, who had accepted more money from the tobacco industry than any other politician, Humanitarian of the Year.

"It is not possible to apply to the human species experimental information derived from *inducing* cancer in animals."

Dr. Kenneth Starr
New South Wales Cancer Council

On a scientific level, leaving out the misery factor, Yellow Fever is one of the infinite major failures of vivisection.

Try as they did, vivisectors could not inflict any animals with the disease. So when Havana, Cuba was ravaged by Yellow Fever, the government asked for human volunteers, and discovered that mosquitoes transmitted the disease. They implemented quarantines and sanitation standards, and Yellow Fever was obliterated.

"The knowledge gained from studies in animals is often not pertinent to human beings, will almost certainly be inadequate, and may even be misleading."

Arnold D. Welch
Yale University Department of Pharmacology

Most carcinogenics that cause cancer have been discovered by clinical and epidemiology studies on humans, not animal experiments. An example of an epidemiology study would be: "Why is colon cancer rare in Japan but common in Europe and North America?" One of the easy tricks for animal researchers is to produce lots of impressive sounding data even if it means nothing, to get more grant money.

"As a cancer specialist engaged in clinical practice, I can't agree with the researchers who believe that results obtained with laboratory animals are applicable to human beings."

Dr. Heinz Oeser

Walter Stewart, a lead investigator for NIH, said that over 25% of the published medical research reports are *outright frauds*, to obtain more of your tax dollars in grant money.

"I have been a surgeon for 51 years. I am still performing operations daily, and can state that in no way whatever do I owe my dexterity to animals experimentation...If I had to learn surgery through animal experiments I would have been an incompetent in this field, just as I consider those of my colleagues to be incompetent who say that they learned surgery through animal experimentation. It's true that there are always advocates of vivisection who say that one must first practice on animals in order to become a surgeon. This is a dishonest statement, made by people who reap FINANCIAL benefit from it."

Dr. Ferndinando de Leo,
Professor of Pathological Surgery, University of Naples

Here's a tiny sample of your animal experiment tax dollars at work, and their stellar discoveries:

Stanford University Vivisectors were paid $150,000 of your tax dollars to collect elderly cats from questionable sources. The researchers locked these elderly cats in very cold rooms for days, then locked them in very warm rooms. The astonishing finding was: "Old cats don't sleep well in very hot or very cold rooms."

Surprise: We need more $$$ to determine why?

"At a time when millions are starving in the world, and our economy is in great trouble, Congress is allocating BILLIONS of dollars annually in grants for basic, no-goal research on LIVING ANIMALS. Careers in torture are as financially rewarding as they are morally bankrupt. Reports in medical journals recorded by the experimenters themselves are indisputable indictments of their gross inhumanity."

Barbara Schultz
Member of New York Attorney General Advisory Committee

Case Western Reserve was reportedly paid $150,000 of your tax dollars to surgically CRIPPLE Labrador retriever PUPPIES. Their wonderful finding after committing this atrocious act was, the puppies suffered weakness and loss of bone mass where their ankles had been crippled by the vivisecting veterinarians.

"Vivisection appeals to the basest instincts of fear and cowardice and is rooted in the unjust principle that might makes right and

28

that the end justifies the means, thus permitting any cruelty on the tyrant's plea of necessity. Because of human justice, vivisection stands condemned on three main courts: cruelty to animals, uselessness to man, and obstruction on the path of true knowledge."

Dr. M. Beddow Baily

Boston University & Yerkes Regional Primate Research Center were paid $1,225,000 of your tax dollars to test old monkeys who had lived a life of psychological experiments, restraining chairs, shocks, etc. Only to discover, old monkeys don't learn as fast as young monkeys. Imagine that! College is the answer!

"A course of experimental physiology in which animals are agonized to exhibit facts already established, is a disgrace to the country that permits it."

Dr. John Elliotson

When vivisectors PR proclaims they treat animals better than most pets, think about some of their routine experiments such as LD50(Lethal Dose 50 percent) product test. The lethal level of a product is measured by force-feeding a number of animals until half of them die, terribly painful and slow deaths as the organs rupture, often from volume rather than toxicity.

"...Moreover, the (animal) tests deceive the very consumers whom they are supposed to protect, by certifying as safe household products and cosmetics that cause nearly 200,000(U.S.)hospital-recorded poisonous exposures annually."

Dr. Paula Kislak

Physicians Committee For Responsible Medicine, Declaration 1988

Most modern vivisectors hide behind the assumption put out by psychologist, B.F. Skinner in 1953, that the study of animals can yield results that will ultimately benefit humans. Skinner said, "We study animals because it's simpler...we can vary states of deprivation over wide ranges," isn't that wonderful. But even he added, "human behavior is inevitably set apart as a separate field." Skinner should

29

have subjected himself to the Skinner Box he kept animals in and even his own daughter; but he, like other vivisectors, never experience the horrors they induce even for a short period of time...

"It is the outrageous lie of the supporters of vivisection, a lie serious in its consequence, that animal experiments take place for the good of mankind. The opposite is the case: animal experiments only have an alibi function for the purpose of obtaining money, power and titles. Not one single animal experiment has ever succeeded in prolonging or improving, let alone saving, the life of even one single person."

Dr. Heide Evers

Many drugs that are beneficial to humans were delayed because they could not pass animal experiments, such as fluoride that caused mouth and bone cancer in rats, the heart drug digitalis, quinine for malaria, the pain killer morphine, ether, sulfanilamide a diuretic, cortisone and aspirin to name just a few. Insulin caused birth defects in chickens, rabbits and mice, but not in man. Morphine sedates man but stimulates cats, aspirin is poison to cats, and useless for horses.

"It is incomprehensible how parties with vested interests repeatedly assert the necessity and purposefulness of animal experiments, paying no regard to the views of many who think otherwise, and at the same time conceal the fact that the defense used against claims for damages resulting from side effects caused by extensively used animal-tested medicaments and chemical substances is precisely that the animal-test results couldn't be applied to the human organism."

Dr. Werner Hartinger

Research lobbyists and PR mills constantly feed the media propaganda as news stories to snag your tax dollars in the form huge research grants so they can continue vivisecting healthy animals, by asserting the similarities between various species and humans far outweighs the differences.

"Ask the experimenters why they experiment on animals, and the answer is: 'Because the animals are like us.' Ask the experimenters why it is morally OK to experiment on animals, and the answer is: 'Because the animals are not like us.' Animal experimentation rests on logical contradiction."

Professor Charles R. Magel

The following is extracted with permission from *The Animals Agenda*, by Roger E. Ulrich. Over a 100 years of animal research may have left our culture further behind in the search for wisdom than when it started.

"(After) I completed my doctoral dissertation entitled, Reflexive Fighting in Response to Aversive Stimulation--shocking rats to get them to fight, I got my Ph.D., and I joined the army of animal researchers who contend that we must conduct further experiments."

"Scientists ask why? But they never ask, SHOULD I?"

Michael Crichton
Author of *Jurassic Park*

A vivisector's confession continues: "Laboratory aggression experiments provide a perfect example of basic research," one animal experiment leads to the next animal experiment to keep the money coming... "with each project following the preceding one as a direct consequence, and with each being essentially as irrelevant to solving real human problems as the one before...with many of my vivisector colleagues agreeing, but that it was of "little consequence to the animals still confined in laboratory cages around the world."

"Vivisection can only be defended by showing it to be right that one species should suffer in order that another species be

31

happier...If we cut up animals simply because they cannot prevent us and because we are backing our own side in the struggle for existence, it's only logical to cut up imbeciles, criminals, enemies, or capitalists for the same reason."

C.S. Lewis
Christian Author

A vivisector's confession continues: He stumbles onto the discovery that even the *cruel theory of shocking* animals like he had been doing for ten years under the guise of studying aggression to help humans...and who wouldn't get angry being shocked with electricity, is based on a 1948 experiment that was itself *contrived* by another vivisector, Neal E. Miller.

"Vivisection is wrong because it is an abuse of man's power over the helpless, involving pain and suffering. The name for this is cruelty, and cruelty is immoral, no matter what the reason for its introduction."

Jon Evans

A vivisector's confession continues: "I helped design new strategies and new equipment for shocking anything that moved, and even observed children whom I convinced to shock some rats and 'watch what happens.'
More and more allegedly new discoveries were added to a voluminous literature(weighing 50 pounds)...all involving countless animals, with the findings essentially irrelevant to people...studies leading to new studies...I was collecting for a book."

"There is a conditioned brutality among scientists."

Dr. Kit Pedler

A vivisector's confession continues: Our renowned researcher talks about being invited as a prestigious guest speaker across America, throughout Europe, Asia, Central and South America, making movies to justify vivisection against animal welfare causes and using his prominence to perpetually apply for grant money from every local, state, federal, private, and public agency to support his vivisection projects.

Excerpt: "The sums that are being spent (on cancer research) are enormous: $600 million ...a year (in 1975) ...Dr. James Watson...who helped discover the molecular structure of life's genetic material, derided the National Cancer Program as a fraud..."

Article: *"Is Cancer Research Worth Cost?"*
London Economist News Service

A vivisector's confession continues: "I came to the conclusion that if the control of human aggression was our goal...we were looking in the wrong place...my own anger was often uncontrollable, despite my discoveries and laboratory knowledge."

"I do not believe that chimpanzees, rats and the rest should be sacrificed, even for an acknowledged greater good; such a sacrifice infringes their right to refuse. In my morality, all creatures with feelings and wishes should be thought of as ends-in-themselves, and not merely means."

Professor Stephen L. Clark

A vivisector's confession continues: "One spring, in response to my department chairman's question, 'What is the most innovative thing that you have done professionally during the past year?' I replied, '...I've finally stopped torturing animals.'"

"The case against vivisection is the same as that against war and all other forms of cruelty--that violence does not produce long term solutions."

Jon Wynne-Tyson

Vivisection is the traditional cruel way of medical research. Changing tradition is never easy. When FDR enacted Child Labor Laws, the right-wing business establishment went nuts, and encouraged the right-wing Supreme Court to repeal them as unconstitutional. Today we have the former Surgeon General C. Everett Koop backing the wealthy vivisectors. "There is no substitute for animal testing if we are to ensure the safety of all consumer products, from personal care and household cleaning products to health care and prescription drugs."

But even one of the largest corporate drug vivisectors with firsthand knowledge admitted: "The weakness and intellectual poverty of a naive trust in animal tests may be shown in several ways; e.g.; the humiliating large number of medicines discovered only by serendipitous observation in man(ranging from diuretics to antidepressants), or by astute analysis of deliberate or accidental(human) poisoning, the notorious examples of valuable medicines which have seemingly 'unacceptable' toxicity in animals, e.g., hepatic necrosis in mice, the stimulant action of morphine in cats, and such instances of unprecedented toxicity in man as the production of pulmonary hypertension which appeared during animal tests.

Because of the often misleading nature of animal experiments this could divert attention from other possible side-effects which may arise. In any case, human trials should involve careful clinical observation whatever animal or alternative tests have indicated."

A.D. Dayan
Wellcome Research Drug Corporation

Christopher Reeve, the likable actor paralyzed from the neck down due to a tragic fall from a horse jumping incident that snapped his spinal cord, gave a heartfelt speech at the 1996 Democratic Convention in Chicago, during which he called for more research for spinal-cord injures. He might have meant to add, non-animal research, but only he knows. He did mention in another interview, growing human cells as holding what he thought was the best hope...

"Maybe paraplegics will be able to get out of wheelchairs someday," said Ingrid Kirkland, Co-founder of PETA, "but it will be from high technical non-animal research, not because some researcher has

34

smashed monkeys' spines."

In September 1996, Mr. Reeve attended the University of California at Irvine spinal injury center bearing his name, to honor a Swiss nerve regeneration researcher. The UC Irvine spinal center is going to be headquarters for worldwide spinal research. Unfortunately, vivisectors smell money when any cause has public sympathy, and unfortunately in most cases *unconsenting* animals will *intentionally* bear the *unnecessary* pain and suffering for research dollars. **Yes to Research. No to animal research.**

"Practocol was prescribed for over 4 years before doctors realized that it caused corneal damage including blindness, a side effect not predicted by animal experiments."

C.T. Dollery
Risk-Benefit Analysis in Drug Research

The University of California is one of many so-called liberal universities, but they are zealous vivisectors, that have been raided for animal abuse (monkeys, cats, etc.), documented in *Free The Animals* and several news stories.

Spinal cord research on animals makes hell look like a vacation retreat. One of many experiments was conducted on cats at Howard University and documented in the book *Free The Animals*

"I would not want to promote research on animals-fortunately, only my back is twisted, not my mind."

Linn Pulis
Polio Victim

Cats had been disappearing in droves around the neighborhoods in the proximity of Howard University. A butcher(cruel animal dealers) had been selling the cats to Howard. By the time The Animal Liberation Front(ALF) rescued the cats, 22 of the 34 cats had already been surgically crippled by the research doctors.

One cat was found dead in his cage. The surgically crippled cats supported themselves on their front legs. Their back legs were spread apart like *frogs legs*, that dragged behind them like dead weights. The thick incisions on their backs looked like a hatchet-man had attacked them then tied the gashes with big black knots.

"Research is subordinated(not to a long-term social benefit)but to an immediate commercial profit. Currently, disease(not health)is one of the major sources of profit...and doctors are willing agents of those profits."

Dr. Pierre Bosquet

I recently received a Cancer Society(ardent vivisectors) colorful glossy mailer, touting the alleged great strides they were making in the $-search-$ for a cure, as they solicited more money.

"I have finally come to the conclusion that no serious importance can be attached to any laboratory experiment on animals... for the results cannot in any circumstances be extrapolated to human beings."

Professor Director Guilio Tarro
Head of Virology & Oncology Medical Faculty of Naples University

"Between 1962 and 1982, the numbers of people who contracted or died of cancer both increased...The bottom line is that despite all the billions of dollars (animal experiments), and the promises and the claims of success, more people are dying of cancer than ever before..." Until voluntary lifestyle changes took place.

Dr. John C. Bailer III
Harvard University of Public Health 1986

Because of the ethical awareness raised by animal welfare groups during the last decades, there is a slow evolution to a higher consciousness taking place. For example, Los Almos labs are now using computers to view and map human thought, Harvard Medical has closed their dog laboratory under student protest, but the cruel science-of-yesterday labs are still thriving and being paid with your tax dollars and government tax credits, to stick painful probes into cats' and monkeys' skulls and worse.

"The atrocities we persist in perpetrating within our laboratories, where scientists are paid to perform painful rituals on other life-forms based on blind faith that human suffering might be driven away, should increasingly be questioned and discontinued. They are not reducing the suffering we so often feel and see around us in the real-life laboratory.

Our addiction to animal research must be given up and replaced with the observation of natural phenomena."

Alan Watts
Author of *Nature, Man and Woman*

Other advances in the spiritual evolution of eliminating animal testing, is that a few judges are becoming aware of the questionable scientific validity of animal experiments, especially for consumer safety, which is causing corporations to re-think their strategy of testing animals to protect themselves in litigation.

"The day may come when the rest of the animal creation may acquire those rights which never could have been withholden from them but by the hand of tyranny."

Jeremy Bentham
Philosopher

One legal discussion was entitled: "The erosion of acceptability of animal toxicity tests in the courtroom," stated that courtroom judges in the U.S. have increasingly found animal data untrustworthy in products liability, which is a major blow to the vivisectors' purse strings should they lose corporate America.

"Until he extends his circle of compassion to all living things,

37

man will not himself find peace."

Dr. Albert Schweitzer

Another area of hope is, that under pressure from animal welfare groups, cosmetic giant Noxell, makers of Noxema, Cover-Girl and other products has adopted the Agarose Diffusion Method, which uses cells rather than rabbits' eyes to tests products and has been very successful in evaluating human responses, in lieu of the sadistic Draize Method which is still used by many companies.

"Most experts agree that animal testing today is virtually pointless. As one clinical director puts it: 'You cannot really rely on tests with any other animal or combination of animals to predict drug or surgical action in man.'"

Curtis Freshel

Your tax dollars at work supplementing cruelty. According to the International Foundation For Science, the United States National Cancer Institute induced tumors in animals for over 25 years then screened over 40,000 species of plants searching for an anti-tumor agent. Several of the plants shrunk tumors in various animals, but most of them did not shrink human tumors, or if they did, proved too toxic for humans and had to be rejected. So after a quarter of a century torturing animals, not one plant was found to be successful treating human tumors.

"The discovery of the law of evolution, which revealed that all organic creatures are of one family, shifted the center of altruism from humanity to the whole conscious world collectively. Therefore, the practice of vivisection has been left by that discovery without any logical argument in its favor."

Thomas Hardy
English Author

The Physicians Committee For Responsible Medicine states that high tech non-animal methods are faster, more accurate, less expensive and would not only eliminate animal suffering but also human suffering of patients waiting years for helpful drugs, if they could convince politicians to stop pandering to wealthy vivisectors who contribute to their campaigns and mislead them.

"Even should it be conclusively proved that human beings benefit directly from the suffering of animals, its infliction would nevertheless be unethical and wrong."

Lord Dowding
Air Chief Marshall

In 1993, Johns Hopkins University organized the first World Congress on Alternatives and Animal Use in Baltimore. About 700 academic, industrial, and research scientists from around the world, as well as government representatives, attended to discuss alternatives to laboratory animal experiments for education, research and safety testing.

"Experts often assert that it is senseless to compare a tumor which has been artificially provoked in an animal with a tumor that has spontaneously developed in a human being."

Dr. Peter Schmidsberger

"Ever occur to you why some of us can be this much concerned with animals suffering? Because the government is not. Why not? Animals don't vote ."

Paul Harvey

Dogs are still the animal of choice in most veterinarian schools. "My lifelong dream and ambition to become a veterinarian dissipated following several traumatic experiences involving standard experimental procedures utilized by the dispassionate instructors of the pre-vet school at my state university. They felt it was perfectly acceptable to experiment with and then terminate the lives of all animals they utilized, which I found revoltingly unacceptable to my own moral code. After numerous confrontations with these heartless vivisectionists, I painfully decided to pursue a different

career."
Former Veterinarian Student Wishing To Remain Anonymous

But for the first time in history there are now medical schools that give students the option, or do not use animals in the training of medical students:

New York University, Ohio State University, University of Michigan, SUNY-Stony Brook, Louisiana State, Howard University, University of Maryland, and now many more universities are allowing students the option of foregoing animal laboratory experiments.

"Nobody has become a surgeon because of having operated on animals. He has only leant wrongly through animals. I have been able to see this over my many decades as a surgeon, and a Director of hospitals. I have carried out tens of thousands of operations on people without ever performing them first on an animal."
Professor Dr. Salvatore Rocca Rossetti
Surgeon & Professor of Urology at the University of Turin, Italy

Some of the many alternatives to animal experiments which eliminate the cruelty and are more reliable are:

In-vitrol studies, which provide fast and precise results because their focus is on cellular and molecular levels of life and can illustrate how chemicals and drugs might help or hurt humans.

Clinical studies of human volunteers, epidemiological (population) studies, human organs, and human autopsies.

Growing human tissue cultures and human cells.

Physico-chemical methods such as liquid chromatographs and mass spectrophotometer that permit scientists to analyze substances in a biological matter rather than ruining thousands of animals' lives.

Computer-aided drug design, such as 3D computer graphics and quantum pharmacology now employed for sickle-cell anemia research to help develop drugs to fight this terrible disease.

40

Genetic engineering, computer simulations, and computer databases to eliminate redundancy and share knowledge.

High tech MRI's, PET's, and CAT scans are more proof, vivisection is the cruel science of the past.

"Computer simulations offer a wide range of advantages over live animal experiments in the physiology and pharmacology laboratory."
Dr. Walker
University of Texas

"Human tissue cultures offer the possibility of studying not only the biology of cancer cell growth and invasion into normal human tissue, but also provide a method for evaluating the effects of a variety of potentially important anti-tumor agents," FDA scientists reported in 1996, after keeping human cells and human tissues alive in cultures for biomedical research, thus avoiding transferring disease which is common when scientist conduct cross-species experiments.

"We have seen that the senses and intuitions, the various emotions and faculties, such as love, memory, attention and curiosity, imitation, reason, etc., of which man boasts, may be found in an incipient, or even sometimes in a well-developed condition, in the lower animals."
Charles Darwin

These advanced non-animal methods are now beginning to be accepted for grant money which is their only hope against the powerful and wealthy vivisectors: doctors, researchers, veterinarians, hospitals, universities and private research facilities, that continue to drain billions of your tax dollars in the form of animal research grants and tax credits, and they will fight hard to scare and mislead the public to keep their money coming.

"...MONEY...is really the difference between men and animals, most of the things men feel, animals feel, and vice versa, but

41

animals do not know about MONEY."

Gertrude Stein
Author

Lobbyist groups for vivisectors might claim otherwise, but according to the Physicians Committee For Responsible Medicine, the following is a short list of medical advances accomplished without animal experiments:

Discovery between cholesterol and heart disease, the number one cause of American deaths.

Discovery between smoking and cancer and nutrition and cancer, the number two cause of American deaths.

Discovery between hypertension and stroke the number three cause of American deaths.

Discovery of the causes of trauma, the number four cause of death in the United States, and how to prevent it.

Elucidation of the multiple forms of respiratory disease, the number five cause of American deaths.

Isolation of the AIDS virus and transmission.

Development of x-rays.

Discovery of penicillin and curative effect on many diseases.

Development of anti-depressant and anti-psychotic drugs.

Development of vaccine against yellow fever.

Discovery of the relationship between chemical exposures and birth defects.

Discovery of human blood groups.

Development of hormonal treatment for cancer in the prostrate and breast.

Discovery of the chemical and physiological visual process in the eye.

Discovery of action of hormones.

Production of Humulin, a synthetic copy of human insulin which causes few allergic reactions.

"There are still people who feel that the rat will guide us to the perfect diet, me, I think it merely guides us to the garbage heap."

Dr. Franklin Bicknell

According to McKinely and McKinely medical researchers from Boston University, 92% of the life expectancy increase from 1900 to 1973 was due to hygiene and lifestyle, and any dramatic declines in mortality occurred before the vaccines and drugs which are usually credited, were even introduced.

"Medicine induced illness has become a public health menace of major and alarming proportions, producing more deaths annually than are caused by breast cancer and ranking among the TOP TEN causes of hospital admissions."

Medicine In Society

The McKinely Study conforms with the Center for Disease Control (CDC) findings, that any rise in life expectancy is from changes in hygiene, lifestyle, and environmental factors not animal research.

"If liberty means anything at all, it means the right to tell people what they do not want to hear."

George Orwell
Author

In 1985, Congress passed an amendment that required vivisectors to exercise dogs and to furnish primates with conditions favorable to their psychological well-being. But under pressure from wealthy vivisectors the USDA made compliance voluntary.

However, a recent token inspection by the USDA of only 16% of the federally funded laboratories, found animal abuse in 80% of them. Yet there were no follow-up or expanded inspections.

"Our task must be to free ourselves...by widening our circle of compassion to embrace all living creatures and the whole of nature and its beauty."

Albert Einstein

When human-mammals are crowded into cramped spaces such as prisons, music concerts or sporting events, violence may erupt.

This is also true with tiny mammals like rodents. Millions of these curious and bright mammals are routinely induced with cancers, drugs, scalded, shocked and maimed. As they wait their experimental fates they are jammed into confined plastic containers where cannibalism sometimes erupts out of frustration.

If the vivisectors were the recipients of the induced diseases, tumors, overdoses, overcrowding, scalding, shocking, maiming experiments, would they have an epiphany....? Fat chance.

"Forgive them, for they know not what they do."
Jesus Christ

Millions of other rodents are subjected to psychological experiments in our finest universities. Water and food are routinely withheld as the students take notes on the deprivation, which has already been documented thousands of times.

Maybe the instructors should volunteer to be deprived of food and water for a couple of days, and have the students take notes on their deprivation, so the instructors may finally comprehend how cruel their experiments are.

"The fate of animals is of greater importance to me than the fear of appearing ridiculous; it is in-dissolubly connected with the fate of men."
Emile Zola
French Author

From 1950 to 1974, vivisectors in West Germany experimented on non-human animals in an attempt to lower human-animal birth defects.

"Only 25 years ago, among every 100,000 children born in the Federal Republic(of West Germany)there were three cases of malformation. Today, five children are malformed for only 1,000 births. Within a quarter of a century, therefore, the malformations have increased more than a hundred-fold...five times as many medicines...and the population is far more frequently ill...Unexpectedly, an industry which was created to heal diseases has become the starting point for
44

new ailments."

Kurt Bluechel
Author of *The White Magicians*

Here is another sample of the insanity, never mind meanness, of testing products and drugs on animals:
Lemons are deadly to cats. So if you wanted to cause havoc to the citrus industry, vivisectors would feed lemons to cats and publish their deadly findings.

Digitalis lowers blood pressure and is extremely valuable to the human-animal's heart, but was postponed for many years because it was ruled dangerous for the heart by vivisectors because it raised the blood pressure of dogs, the animal sacrificed in the experiments.

Novalgin is an anesthetic for the human-animal but speeds cats up almost into convulsions.

Cycloserin is a great aid for tuberculosis in the human-animal, but was tested on guinea-pigs and rats and had no effect on these animals artificially induced with the disease.

Phenyl-butazone the anti-inflammatory drug is poisonous to the human-animal in large doses, but had no effect on the dogs and other lab animals that were administered much higher doses.

Chloramphenicol dangerously damages the blood-producing bone marrow on the human-animal, but the had no affect on the marrow of the lab animals tested.

Chlorpromazine damages the human-animal's liver, but had passed animal testing by several lab animals suffering no damaging effects.

Acidium oroticum aids the human-animal's heart, but because it caused fat to develop on the liver of rats was delayed for several years.

"Various species of animals react differently to the same drug. Not only do the variations in the metabolism of a drug make it difficult to extrapolate results of animal experiments to man but they cre-

45

ate a serious obstacle to the development of new therapeutic drugs."

Dr. Barnard B Brodie
Clinical Pharmacology & Therapeutics

Amanita Mushroom is deadly to human-animals but rabbits thrive on it.

Even the smell of prussic acid will kill a human-animal but toads and sheep love it.

Parsley will kill a parrot.

Opium, even in large chunks, has no effect on porcupines.

Botulin will poison the human-animal but cats thrive on it, but it will kill mice instantly.

Methyl-alcohol will blind the human-animal, but not harm the eyes of most animals experimented on.

Arsenic is poisonous to the human-animal even in small quantities, but sheep can devour enormous quantities.

The human-animal, monkey, and guinea-pigs will develop scurvy if deprived of vitamin C; but dogs, cats, rats, mice, and hamsters will stay healthy because their systems manufacture their own vitamin C.

Just five milligrams of scopolamine can kill the human-animal, but dogs and cats can eat a hundred milligrams with no effect.

Strychnine will kill the human-animal, but have no effect on monkeys, guinea-pigs, or chickens.

Hemlock will kill the human-animal, but sheep, goats, and horses love it.

Amylnitrate lowers the eye pressure in the human-animal, but gravely raises the internal pressure of a dog's eye.

Methyl Fluoroactetate is poisonous to the human-animal

and other mammals, but laboratory rats tolerated forty times the amount the laboratory dogs tolerated before succumbing...

So vivisectors can always manipulate the answer they need to snag your tax dollars to continue their funding, by selecting the pertinent animal for further studies are needed $$$.

"...On account of the dissimilarity between animals and human beings, it is worse than useless to attempt to base any methods of treatment or prevention of human disease on animal experimentation."

Dr. M. Beddow Baily

VIVISECTORS MOUNT A NEW FRONT
Intensely watching the public opinion tide shifting, as millions of animal experiments continue(and abuses continue, like PETA finding dead primates from dehydration at a laboratory funded with your tax dollars; their feet had become jammed in the cage bars and they were unable to reach their water), vivisectors have banded together like never before with patriotic sounding names like "Americans For..." to defend their livelihoods by launching media blitz propaganda campaigns, painting people against cruelty to animals as eccentric nuts and themselves as the medical saviors ever-searching for better human health, as they rush helter-skelter ahead to capture millions of your tax dollars in grant money for their new Frankenstein frontier: CROSS SPECIES TRANSPLANTATION: Vivisectors call: XENOTRANSPLANTATION.

Excerpt: The Guardian Newsletter, Summer 1997: "Organ Xenotransplatation's Track Record: 100% Failure. Fifty-five animal-to-human whole organ transplants, resulting in the suffering and death of all patients and donor animals. Thousands of cross-species experiments since 1906(animal to animal)has not provided reliable information....Over 20 known potentially lethal viruses can be transmitted from non-human primates to humans...pig retroviruses have infected human kidney cells in vitro and the influenza virus of 1918 that killed 20 million was a mutated swine flu virus...The myth of breeding safe *Germ-Free* animals..."

"The excuse of toleration of cruelty upon any living creature by a woman is a deadly sin against the grandest force in nature— maternal love...In not one single instance known to science has the cure of any human disease resulted necessarily from this fallacious method of research."

Dr. Elizabeth Blackwell
Physician & Hospital Administrator

Organ transplantation means killing healthy animals to transplant their organs, tissues, or cells to human-animals.

"Vivisection is mostly undertaken in the expectation that the goal which has been mentally erected is attainable. The results never justify the means as erecting goals is an idle pursuit, as evidence by research conducted on these lines retarding instead of advancing progress."

James McDonagh FRCS

Cross-species organ transplants don't work, because one species NATURally rejects organs from another species, such as baboons, chimpanzees, and pigs. Even organs transplanted from the same species may be rejected to a lesser degree.

"Doctors who speak out in favor of vivisection do not deserve any recognition in society, all the more so since their brutality is apparent not only during such experiments, but also in their practical medical lives. They are mostly men who stop at nothing in order to satisfy their ruthless and unfeeling lust for honors and gain."

Dr. Hugo Knecht
Ear, Nose & Throat Specialist

A vivisectionist reported this year that he had combined human and primate DNA in hopes of producing a super-intelligent primate for slave labor or organ transplants... shades of Aldous Huxley's (human-cloning) *Brave New World*.

"For me, the scientific attraction to animal research had, in the final analysis, little to do with a demonstrable relationship of research findings to the goal of helping humans. In retrospect, I would say the main attraction to working with animals was, as Skinner proclaimed, 'that we can control...'"

Confessions of a Former Vivisector

According to the Physicians For Responsible Medicine, organ transplants can never work unless potent drugs are administered to suppress a person's immune system from rejecting the animal's organ, tissue, or cells.

This means the person no longer has their normal immune system, so will be vulnerable to a myriad of diseases.

Even more dangerous is the transplanted organ, tissues, or cells may also carry more cross-species diseases like AIDS.

"There is the true joy in life; being used for a purpose recognized by yourself as a mighty one, and being a force of nature instead of a feverish, selfish, clod."

George Bernard Shaw

According to an Associated Press article on an Arizona laboratory experimenting with cryobiology for organ transplants: "Cheers erupted..." as the vivisector held a beating rat's heart that had thawed, after pulling it out of the now dead animal. Your tax dollars at work.

"Vivisection is barbaric, useless, and a hindrance to scientific progress."

Dr. Werner Hartinger

Further down the AP article: "'A lot of people get diseases through kidney and liver transplants,' said Dr. Grant Knight, a biochemist at the University of Otago in Dunedin, New Zealand."

Cancer is inadvertently transmitted in 65 of every 150,000 (human never mind animal) organ transplants, according to Joel Newman of the United Network for Organ Sharing, a federally funded entity...

HIV, the virus that causes AIDS, has been passed onto two organ recipients in the last decade, said Joel Newman.

"What I think about vivisection is that if people admit that they have the right to take or endanger the life of living beings for the benefit of many, there will be no limit for their cruelty."

Leo Tolstoy

Excerpt: Los Angeles Time , *Transplant Rules Focus On Animal Viral Risks*.

The President, recognizing the potential in the new experimental field of animal-to-human transplants, proposed strict safeguards...against the transmission of serious animal viruses and other microbes into people."

Further down this LA Times article: "The human immuno-deficiency virus that causes AIDS, for example, is believed to have somehow jumped from African monkeys (vivisection experiments?) into humans through food contamination or during slaughter (after a life of experiments?)."

"Truth is simple. Yet the AIDS virus theory has entered a realm of scientific obfuscation. Our Addiction To Animal Research provides us with faulty information about AIDS and drugs intended for humans, who differ physiologically from other species."

Dr. Laurence E. Badgley 1988
His Forward To The Book: *AIDS* 1988

VIVISECTORS PUSH ORGAN TRANSPLANTS

Excerpt: Time Magazine, Special Issue, with their abysmal

record in tow, vivisectors using Time Magazine, plow forward touting animal organ transplants: "Xenografts. Virtually everyone in the field says greater use of animal-organ transplants," is the way to go, despite the potential for more AIDS-like epidemics to be transplanted...

"The fight against vivisection is a matter of what is right and of moral evolution, an ethical requirement, and as such a question for the whole people."

Dr. Max Bachem

Time Magazine went on to proclaim: Vivisectors started with (killing) baboons, but have moved onto (killing) dogs, mice, monkeys, and pigs at Boston's Pharmacy and Health Sciences at Northeastern University, the Transplant Center at the University of Alabama, and UCLA's heart-transplant program as well as other research centers.

"Modern medicine is a negation of health. It isn't organized to serve human health, but only itself, as an institution. It makes more people sick than it heals."   Ivan Illich

Medical Historian

The whole purpose of Medical PR is to keep the money coming in by schmoozing the public, so vivisectors can secure millions of your tax dollars slated for their pet projects, such as the hot new organ transplant field, so they can continue torturing and killing animals into the foreseeable future. The key to how the PR spins, is always the vested interest who funded ($$$) the research...

"Economics and politics simply intertwine in shaping conventional medicine's approach... treating disease is enormously profitable, preventing disease is not."

British Cancer Control Society

CHIMERISM is what vivisectors call their new twist on Xenografts (organ transplants). After they cage, experiment, then kill thousands of perfectly healthy animals that had a right to their own lives, they transplant the animal's bone marrow and the animal's organ to a sick person, and so that the person won't reject the organ, they suppress the sick person's immune system with new immune suppression drugs.

"About 15,000 new mixtures and dosages hit the market each year, while about 12,000 die off...We simply don't have enough diseases to go around. At the moment the most helpful contribution is the new drug to counteract the untoward effect of other new drugs."

Dr. Walter Modell

"Nine-tenths of our sickness can be prevented by right thinking plus right hygiene...nine-tenths of it!"

Henry Miller
Author In His Old Age

The new wrinkle on this dark theory of transplanting the animal bone marrow with the animal organ is supposedly to cut down on the use of the new immune suppression drugs that leave the already sick person without any immune system...which may prolong the suffering for months at an enormous financial expense before the patient probably succumbs, leaving their family financially and emotionally devastated...And transplanting animal bone marrow with the animal organ, is filled with even more danger to unknown cross-species diseases.

"Every month, millions are in fact being damaged by treatment which is supposed to be helping them."

Dr. Werner Lehmpfuhl

How many thousands of people from Animal Organ Transplants, will have their suffering prolonged and their finances depleted? How many thousands or millions of dogs, mice, monkeys,

52

and pigs will meet their grim fates?

"The oil lobby, perhaps the most powerful lobby on earth, is almost matched by hospital owners and doctors."

President Jimmy Carter

As cynical as it sounds... in some cases, when you go to your private doctor, it's his/her $-business-$ to find something wrong with you. When you go to your HMO (Health Maintenance Organization)it's their $-business-$ to find nothing expensive wrong with you.

"Science...has established a new set of values, which amounts to the pitiless exploitation of the rest of nature for the physical benefit of man."

John Vyvyan

Near the end of the Time Magazine Organ Transplant article, beneath the Time's caption A Hero's Epiphany, under a smiling vivisector's face, there was one medical dissenting voice:
(Transplantation) "is an admission of our failure to deal with the underlying diseases. I would like to see the day when we don't need transplantation," said Dr. Peter Libby of Harvard Medical School.

"A medical profession founded on the callousness to the pain of the other animals may eventually destroy its own sensibility to the pain of humans."

Brigid Brophy
Author

The Time's article relates that successful animal bone marrow and animal organ transplants is of course years and thousands of tortures away from human failure, so that means that smiling vivisectors need more studies $$$$ to continue their work at the expense of other beings.

"The heart of the matter is that some people like to cause

53

injury or death to living things. And many of those who do not are indifferent to those who do."

Norman Cousins

The Time's articles even cited the Institute of Medicine in Washington, recommending to raise colonies of swine as spare parts for the human-animal.

"Today's medicine is at the end of the road. It can no longer be transformed, modified, readjusted. That's been tried too often. Today's medicine must DIE in order to be reborn. We must prepare its complete renovation."

Dr. Maurice Delort

"We have a special duty to all animals and we must fight against the merchants of animal suffering who subordinate compassion to the heartless demands of so-called scientific progress."

Edgar Lustgarten

Decades from now society may cringe in horror at the barbarism of vivisection, the same as we wince in disbelief at the old medical treatments for head pain, such as drilling holes in the patient's head to let out demons, or bloodletting to drain out diseases.

"At present scientists do not look for alternatives simply because they do not care enough about the animals they are using."

Peter Singer
Author

Human organ and tissue drives, similar to blood drives, should drastically reduce the need to venture any further into this Frankenstein science; but maybe vivisectors' careers, based on the exploitation and suffering of other lives, might be the real driving force behind their PR.

"If, as we know, the creatures with fur, feathers or fins are

54

our brothers in a lower stage of development, then their very weakness and inability to protest demands that man should refrain from torturing them for the mere possibility of obtaining some knowledge which he believes may be to his own interests."

Lurther Burbank
Philosopher/Horiculturis

According to many leading scientists without a vested interest in vivisection, gene-therapy-non-animal-research offers the most hope for diseases such as cancer, but the bulk of the research grant money goes to animal researchers who are always using the media and celebrities or their families unfortunately stricken with some affliction, to do their PR bidding for more animal research, but they always leave out that it is animal research, and animals will be tortured. And vivisectors will always slant the statistics in their favor to keep the money coming in. **Research Yes; animal research NO.**

If ANIMAL RESEARCH were banned tomorrow, researchers who claim ANIMALS are necessary would discover ANIMALS are not NECESSARY.

"...The simple unadulterated truth is that they(vivisectors)are neither winning the fight against cancer nor are they about to find a cure. They have been claiming that a cure is just around the corner for a good 50 years or more, but the sad fact remains that in spite of the countless millions being collected, cancer in its most serious forms-in the lung, breast and bowel-is no nearer to being beaten today than it was at the turn of the century. Indeed, in some cases-breast for example-the exact opposite is true; the scientists are actually losing the fight." And so are the animals.

Cancer Control Society, Great Britain 1986

According to a study published by the Associated Press, a dangerous pig virus thousands of years old has been found in the DNA of seemingly healthy pigs, and may be passed to humans through pig-to-human organ transplants.

"I don't want to be an alarmist but I do think the transplant surgeons ought to know about our work," said Robin Weiss, one of the scientist reporting the work from the Institute of Cancer Research in London. "The new work shows that such infection is 'more plausible than a fanciful scare .'"

"Nobody knows how many of these viruses exists," said the AP article. "Their genes are usually inactive in pigs, and if they do produce new viruses, the germs appear harmless to animals."

The AP article concluded near the end: "Joe Allan, a virus expert at the Southwest Foundation for Biomedical Research in San Antonio, who has been outspoken about risks of infection from animal tissue, said he thought animal-to-human transplant should be banned until they're proven safe."

According to the American Anti-Vivisection Society (AAVS):

"Virtually everything has been tested on animals at some point, even many time-tested, natural ingredients which have been in use for centuries. The fact that some companies have made the unfortunate decision to test these clearly safe ingredients on animals, does not mean that those using these ingredients are supporting the animal testing industry.

Some companies use new ingredients which have been tested in the relatively recent past. Some use a five year rule, not using any ingredients tested within the previous five years. Others may have a longer period of time which they allow between animal testing, and the use of an ingredient. It is important to note that for ingredients which have been in use for years, the fact that animal tests have been done in the past is irrelevant.

It is years of human data which have assured the safety of these products. Individuals must determine for themselves how much time passing between animal testing and use of ingredients, constitutes support of the practice of animal experimentation.

The issue is further complicated by the fact that some companies don't perform animal experiments themselves, but contract other companies to test products, or purchase the data obtained by other companies conducting animal tests of ingredients.

Additionally, some companies may conduct animal tests for many of their products, but also produce some products using natural ingredients which they do not test. These may be labeled cruelty-free. Again, individuals must determine whether their consumer pressure is to be directed at the product or the producer."

For the latest shopping list of cruelty-free companies, please send $3.50 to Foley Publishing, PO Box 32, Port Costa, CA 94569. All orders are shipped within 24-hours.

A percent of the net income is donated to various Animal Welfare Causes. For donation information, please send a separate SASE with your request.

Photos Obtained in 1999

BEFORE   **DURING**

This particular hideous and useless *Cat Brain Experiment (supposedly to study sense of balance),* has been conducted for over 36-years at Rockefeller University, with documented millions of your tax dollars. A network of similar tests are now being conducted with your tax dollars at other fine institutions across the U.S.

Formerly playful and healthy kittens are locked into stereotoxic frames; electrodes are inserted into their brains and transducers throughout their bodies; then their lungs are collapsed.

If they are still alive after a battery of *tests,* their heads are cemented to computer-driven-head-rotators and their bodies are suspended by hip pins and a spinal clamp, then their backs are carved opened, so their exposed spinal cords can be electronically zapped...the *paralyzed preparations* (cats) are then mutilated...

Then other formerly playful and healthy kittens are locked into stereotoxic frames...

Presurred by the EPA(Environmental Protection Agency) Al Gore, announced fast-track chemical testing for the EPA. The EPA claimed that after decades of subjecting thousands of animals to angonizing and useless testing, such as the *lethal-dose-test*, where groups of animals are force-fed or forced-to-inhale chemicals until half of them die, they still did not have enough data to verify if chemicals such as: turpentine, lead, and rat poison are poisonous.

BEFORE

AFTER

An *abraded-skin-chemical-test,* where the skin is made raw, then poisonous, burning chemicals are rubbed in.

COSMETIC TESTING

BEFORE

AFTER..
And Continuously Until Blind Or Dead.

INCISION-RIDDLED BABOON

Despite decades of lip-service, Procter & Gamble continues painful operations and redundant animal testing for their household, personal care, and pharmaceutical product testing. Thousands of animals are killed each year in Procter & Gamble laboratories.

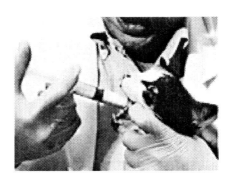

Pharmaceutical Testing

REPULSIVE SLEEP DEPRIVATION STUDIES

Since 1933, $45 million of your tax dollars has been used to torture dogs, cats, monkeys and other animals to study *sleep deprivation.*

Electrodes are placed into their brains, wires are sewn into their hearts, thermometers are surgically buried in their stomachs, and catheters are run through their jugular veins. In this particular study, every time the cat attempts to dose off, he is shocked awake.

In another current *sleep deprivation* study, cats are forced to walk treadmills until they collapse and die of exhaustion. Animals endured these two nightmares-from-hell for 11 to 32 days before dying of exhaustion.

The University of Chicago is the current leader, but by no means the only animal laboratory conducting these sadistic studies.

FACTORY FARMING FOR GAIN

"The greatness of a nation and its moral progress can be judged by the way its animals are treated."

Gandhi

Factory farming is not the idyllic family farm of the past that is still falsely portrayed in advertising. Factory farming is industrial farming: mass producing non-human animals at a maximum output and profit margin as end products: eggs, meat, leather, etc.

Expenses are often slashed to the barest minimum by feeding the living animals carcasses of slaughtered animals, confining the animals to cramped quarters in unnatural settings, and not providing bedding (or leaving soiled bedding).

"The major cruelties practiced on animals in civilized countries today arise out of commercial exploitation, and the fear of losing profits is the chief obstacle to reform."

C.W. Hume

Factory farming also includes the breeding of caged laboratory animals because they too are mass produced, then housed in unnatural, crowded and often poor conditions before and during their experimentation.

"There is an apparent lack of routine health screening procedures, to screen for chronic infections and parasitism, and a lack of adequate patient pre-treatment screening procedures...This alone demonstrates exceedingly poor science and would make data so generated suspect."

Dr. Bernard F. Feldman

Even though parlaying animal testing results to humans is extremely inaccurate; livestock, poultry, cats and dogs continue to have pesticides force-fed and/or are forced to inhale the chemicals in long term experiments, to determine if the pesticides cause cancer.

The animals subjected to these horrific force-feeding experiments suffer blood oozing from their eyes, noses, mouths and rectums. Their internal organs usually ulcerate from the massive overdose of chemicals, and often gag, go into convulsions, and become paralyzed before slipping into comas or die painful deaths from poison overdoses.

"But for the sake of some little mouthful of flesh we deprive a soul the sun and light, and that proportion of life and time it had been born into the world to enjoy."

Plutarch
Greek Philosopher

The futility of animal experimentation is that any chemical, drug, or procedure tested on animals, has to be re-tested on humans.

"I hope to make people realize how totally helpless animals are, how dependent on us, trusting as a child must that we will be kind and take care of their needs...(They)are an obligation put on us, a responsibility we have no right to neglect, nor to violate by cruelty."

James Herriot
Author/Veterinarian

The herbicide dioxin passed the cruelty of animal testing but is now linked with causing human arthritis, birth defects, impaired immune systems, testicular and breast cancer. Dioxin can still be found in some milk cartons, coffee filters, and other bleached paper products.

"The only thing we have to fear on this planet is man."

Carl Jung

Residues from an estimated 1.5 billion pounds of pesticides, herbicides and fungicides sprayed annually by U.S. farmers can be detected in 50% of our food. *All of which passed animal testing*, but is now associated with *cancer* and other serious health problems.

Government inspections have detected over seventeen different pesticides in ground water in twenty-three states. Lawn and tree pesticides are now also being linked as probable carcinogens to various cancers.

"Government cannot close its eyes to the pollution of waters, to the erosion of soil, to the slashing of forests any more than it can close its eyes to the need for slum clearance and schools."

FDR

Professor Stephen Beaumont from the University of Arizona and co-author of *The Forgotten Pollinators*, was featured on the *Osgood Files* radio commentary. He stated that 75% of the crops that feed the world rely on bee pollination, but from "pesticide overuse and the destruction of wildlands," the bee colonies have been destroyed, along with birds, moths and other needed insects, and that in the "last two years we have seen the failures of commercial pumpkin crops," from what he called the "pollination crisis," which was predicted and laughed at decades earlier by Rachel Carson, if we continued heavy pesticide use.

"Silent springs followed by fruitless falls."

Rachel Carson
Author & Environmentalist

The Associated Press reported that deformed frogs, "missing or shrunken eyes, stumps for legs, as many as four tangled hind legs, smaller sex organs," and other mutations were showing up across Minnesota, Wisconsin, South Dakota, Quebec and Vermont. Scientists are speculating the mutations are from pesticides, radiation from ozone depletion, parasites, retinoids or a *combination* of factors.

"There's a reasonable assumption that if there's an external substance influencing amphibian development, it could influence human development," said David Hoppe, a scientist researching the (deformed frogs)problem.

In *factory farming* the animals lives are continually manipulated through chemicals, antibiotics, growth hormones, drugs, breeding, feeding and confines to lay more eggs faster, become fatter quicker, or make leaner meat that human-animals eventually eat.

One of Leonardo Da Vinci's 16 century visions was helicopters. Some of his other predictions are more disturbing:
"Nothing will be left, nothing in the air, nothing under the earth, nothing in the waters. All will be exterminated."

Leonardo Da Vinci

The drugs and hormones used to speed up and amplify meat production may also be dangerous for human consumption. Studies have found the copious amounts of antibiotics fed to animals may breakdown the human immune system, and leave meat-eaters open to bacterial diseases which may become resistant to antibiotic treatment.

"The majority of diseases which the human family have been and still are suffering under, they have created by ignorance of their own organic health, and work perseveringly to tear themselves to pieces, and when broken down and debilitated in body and mind, send for the doctor and drug themselves to death."

Ellen White
Founder Seventh Day Adventists

Battery-hen production is one of the most well know factory farming procedures: Rows of tiny cages containing thousands of confined hens are stacked on top of each other inside a barn. Typically up to five birds, each having an average wingspan of thirty-two inches are cramped into cages twenty inches wide.

"I am sometimes asked, 'Why do you spend so much time and money talking about kindness to animals when there is so much cruelty to men?' I answer: 'I am working at the roots.'"

George T. Angell

The hens are painfully de-beaked and sometimes de-clawed because of the overcrowded quarters. The de-beaking takes place once or twice in their lives.

The first time is at one day old and then again at about seven weeks old if the beak grows back. De-beaking is done with a hot machine knife that painfully burns through the highly sensitive thick tissue between the horn and bone of the beak.

After de-beaking the hen has great difficulty eating and drinking.

"If a man aspires towards a righteous life, his first act of abstinence is from injury to animals."

Leo Tolstoy

The tiny hen cages have no floors so the hens live their cramped lives standing on wire mesh which deforms their feet.

They are never allowed out, never allowed to perch, ground-scratch, dust-bathe or nest. Because of the artificial conditions such as continuous summer light and manipulated diets, the hens continue to lay eggs even when gravely injured.

After their distressed lives in solitary confinement, they are slaughtered.

"The recklessness with which we sacrifice our sense of decency to maximize profit in the factory farming process sets a pattern for cruelty to our own kind."

Jonathan Kozol
Author

Even in well intentioned free-range farms, many of which are enormous barns with access to the outside, there is a major drawback: many hens never wager out, because the light and food are inside.

"One of the remarks made by farmers at their public discussion of these problems suggest that they are rapidly ceasing to think of animals as sentient beings at all. If you handle vast numbers of creatures which are in any case going to die soon, it is, I suppose, easy to get into a state of mind in which they seem to be merely machines."

Kingsley Martin

In factory farming male chickens are killed by the millions; either by stuffing them in plastic bags on top of each other to suffocate, or by crushing, gassing, drowning or killing them by other economical means.

In comparison to the millions of males killed, only a few males are raised for food, if deemed profitable. Those selected males will then meet the fate of a slaughtered hen; after her machine-gun-like egg-laying life is over... they will hang with her upside down on a conveyor line with their heads dragging through an electrified water trough, then their throats will be slit as they are dragged through scalding water...even at this point, some are still fluttering and squealing in pain.

"It is only by softening and disguising dead flesh by culinary preparation, that it is rendered susceptible of mastication or digestion; and that the sight of its bloody juices and raw horror does not excite intolerable loathing and disgust."

Percy Bysshe Shelley

Free-range hens are usually slaughtered after two years, when their productivity declines. Their normal life span is about five to seven years.

Eggs also are a main carrier of salmonella poisoning.

"Farm animals can be kept five to a cage; two-feet-square, tied up constantly by a two-foot-long tether, castrated without anesthesia, or branded with a hot iron. A pet owner would be no less than prosecuted for treating a companion animal in such a manner; an American president was, in fact, morally censured merely for pulling the ears of his two beagles."

Michael W. Fox
Vice President of the Human Society of United States

Many holidays have the catch-22 of celebrating life, by killing, cooking, then eating *dead* animals...

"I have no doubt that it is a part of the destiny of the human race, in its gradual improvement, to leave off eating animals."

Henry David Thoreau

Turkey farming these days, like the meat and dairy industry, is a behemoth Agribusiness. Butterball Turkey is a division of ConAgra Turkey Co., which is a division of ConAgra Poultry Co., which is a division of ConAgra, Inc., and so on...

"Animal factories are one more sign of the extent to which our technological capacities have advanced faster than our ethics."

Jim Mason
Actor

Turkeys have only been domesticated for about a century. In the wild, turkeys lay only a few eggs, called *going broody* once a year. But because of artificial insemination, modern turkey farming deceives the turkeys into continuously laying eggs.

"Few people are capable of expressing with equanimity opinions which differ from that of their social environment."

Albert Einstein

A typical hen-barn contains thousands of white breeding hens. Usually the flock is separated by metal *nests* down the middle of the building. A conveyor belt carries the eggs from the nests.

Insemination occurs once or twice a week. Men called *drivers* herd about fifty to a hundred hens to one side of the barn, then drive a handful of the hens into a chute and force them into a concrete pit, called the *belly*.

In the belly, the herders *break* the terrified hens, by dragging her legs into the pit, then holding her breast and crossed legs down to force her tail to raise up, so the *inseminator* can insert the tube into her cloaca and shoot in semen mixed with antibiotics-- all this terror in less than twelve seconds. Insemination crews are rough and callous. They are pushed to inseminate up to six hundred hens per hour.

"It is a man's sympathy with all creatures that first makes him truly a man."

Dr. Albert Schweitzer

The breeding *tom* turkeys don't have it any better. About four hundred toms live in a house, twenty to each pen. They are

70

usually *milked* about twice a week. The tom is chased down and wrestled onto a bench. He is held upside down by the legs, then his crossed feet and legs are locked into a padded clamp, and his legs are jerked up over his neck and head. The tom's vent is squeezed open by a *handset* until a couple of drops of semen seep out into a glass tube that already has antibiotics in it.

"Cruelty is the vice most natural to dullness of mind."
H.W. Nevinson

Turkey farmers balloon the breeding toms up to seventy pounds, and after about a year-and-a-half when they're done breeding them, the toms are slaughtered with the breeding hens for pet food, lunch meat, soup and pot pies.

"We have enslaved the rest of animal creation, and have treated our distant cousin in fur and feathers so badly that beyond doubt, if they were able to formulate a religion, they would depict the *Devil* in human form."
William Ralph Inge
Clergyman & Author

Pig production is another popular factory farming method. The pigs are cramped into concrete pens without straw or earth. They can only move a few inches... industrial ranchers say this method provides the best *pork*.

When the adult pig called a *sow* has a litter, the only contact her piglets have with her is through dividers, so they can suck her nipples called *teats*. They are kept separate and not allowed to sleep with mom.

"True benevolence, or compassion, extends itself through the whole of existence and sympathizes with the distress of every creature capable of sensation."
Joseph Addison
English Essayist
71

Calf production is also a very restrictive process. The baby calves are taken from their mothers at one to three days old. The least healthy calves are taken on a distressing trip to be slaughtered for pet food, pies, and rennet for cheese. Some of the females become dairy herd replacements.

The rest of the calves are sold at market and spend their lives alone in dark and narrow five by two foot crates that barely allow them room to stand or lie down, but not enough room to turn. To keep them pale and anemic, they are fed only liquid diets without iron or fiber. Even bedding is sometimes withheld, because the calves are so hungry they might eat it.

After three to five months the calves are slaughtered and become the delicacy called *veal*. Many calves die before they are slaughtered, from malnutrition and poor conditions.

"If you have just dined, and however scrupulously the slaughterhouse is concealed in the graceful distance of miles, there is complicity."

Ralph Waldo Emerson
Author & Philosopher

On the surface, cattle farming may seem kind in comparison to factory farming. But cattle farming is taking its toll on six continents. Besides clear cutting rain forests which supply oxygen, and destroying habitats into extinction for pasture land, overgrazing the government subsidized land is the major cause of topsoil erosion.

"Nature to be commanded must be obeyed."

Francis Bacon

Conservationists report that from 1967 and 1975, an estimated two-thirds of the seventy million acres of lost forests went to grazing. The U.S. has lost approximately 75% of its topsoil, and 85% of that is directly linked to livestock grazing. Overgrazing is the main cause

72

of manmade deserts, which can no longer grow crops or support plant life.

"Such prosperity as we have known it up to the present is the consequence of rapidly spending the planet's irreplaceable capital."

Aldous Huxley

The cattle industry argues it has replaced some grazing with their *feedlot paradigm*. This means the cattle are fed with grains and corns for their final fattening before slaughter. The feedlot paradigm does reduce some grazing but is a wasteful way to use crops, because it takes sixteen times the amount of crops to fatten cattle, than if a person ate the crops directly. An estimated 80% of the corn and 95% of the oats grown in the U.S. are now fed to livestock.

"We plow under habitats of other animals to grow hybrid corn that fattens our genetically engineered animals for slaughter. We make free species extinct and domesticate species into bio-machines. We build cruelty into our diet."

Jim Mason

Up to six billion sensitive animals are unnecessarily slaughtered each year. Anybody who has witnessed the slaughterhouse process knows the stress and horror the animals experience; knows the animals are terrified; knows the animals suffer greatly; and knows the painless slaughterhouse is a fantasy. Modern meat production has not eliminated suffering.

"I grew up in cattle country—that's why I became a vegetarian. Meat stinks, for the animals, the environment, and your health."

k.d. lang
Musician

73

The freight train to the slaughterhouse is usually a long journey. The animals are herded into crowded boxcars. Food and water are withheld during transport.

The animals are electrically stunned in the slaughterhouse to comply with the Humane Slaughter Act, but when hens are slaughtered they not covered by the Act so they are not even stunned. But when the human-animal is administered much lower voltage electric shock therapy they are anesthetized, *because electricity is painful.*

"Animals are my friends...and I don't eat my friends."

George Bernard Shaw

Animals slaughtered under Kosher conditions apparently meet even a crueler fate. These animals are very conscious as they are hoisted up in the air, which frequently ruptures the joints as they slowly and painfully bleed to death.

"A man is really ethical only when he obeys the constraint laid on him to aid all life which he is able to help, and when he goes out of his way to avoid injuring anything living. He does not ask how far this or that life deserves sympathy as valuable in itself, not how far it is capable of feeling. To him life as such is sacred..."

Dr. Albert Schweitzer

The pole-axe used in the traditional slaughter is suppose to deliver one death blow, but the slaughterhouse workers often need more than one fatal blow to kill the animal; as the waiting animals nervously drool, frantically moo and lumber about chaotically in close quarters, relieving themselves...waiting their fates.

"I always assumed slaughterhouses were *now* painless. But after smelling the sickening stench of death wafting out before I even entered the dank and dimly lit slaughterhouse, then witnessing the awesome fear and pain first hand, and hearing the fear the animals feel first hand, fighting for their lives to get out of the conveyor-belt process while being goaded with electric prods to keep them moving to the waiting chutes; then violently prodding them into an enclosed steel killing-shed with the thrashing animal gazing pitifully towards the no-way-out ceiling, there's no question these animals know what's coming, as they smell the pools of blood and dead flesh...before they feel the pneumatic nail gun fire against their skulls...The whole cruel process made me so sick, I haven't eaten meat since."

Sergeant Barry Moore, U.S. Army
First and Last Visit to a Slaughterhouse

"It is incredible how much prejudice has been allowed to operate in favor of (flesh)meat, while so many facts are opposed to the pretended necessity of its use."

Philippe Hecquet

Modern techno-dairy farming also classifies as factory farming. Since the 1950s the misery of cows has been greatly intensified, as her output has increased by five fold.

"People often say that humans have always eaten animals, as if this is a justification for continuing the practice. According to this logic, we should not try to prevent people from murdering other people, since this has also been done since the earliest of times."

Isaac Bashevis Singer

Calves are taken from their mothers at only a few days old, fed drugs, hormones, and extremely high protein diets. Cows are milked for about ten months straight, to produce ten times the normal amount of milk. The cows frequently develop mastitis (inflammation of the udder), acidosis, lameness, and by about five years old they are worn out and slaughtered. A cows normal lifespan is approximately twenty years.

"Family organization is broken and young animals are increasingly being denied a mother to turn to for comfort and for grooming. One of the saddest and most pathetic farm practices—inevitable at the present time for the supply of dairy produce—is the separation of the calf from the cow at birth or soon after."

Ruth Harrison

The transition from a meat eating to a vegetarian society is a gradual evolution process, as would be the economic transfer for those employed in that industry, like many other industries in transformation.

"The hormones they give our animals give us cancer."

Burton Goldburg, CEO for Alternative Medicine Magazine
Author of Alternative Medicine Definitive Guide

Slavery was a profitable industry that was always morally wrong, but only after great outcries and sacrifice by the abolitionists raising consciousness did the slave trade became illegal. There is always resistance to change. And a price to be paid.

"Nothing is more powerful than an individual acting out of his conscience, thus helping to bring the collective conscience to life."

Norman Cousins

The Bible was used to justify slavery's morality, as the Bible is used to abuse animals. Those is favor of the status quo treatment of animals now use the Bible, Book of Genesis 1 "Let them have *dominion* over the fish of the sea, and over the fowl of the air, and over the cattle, and over all the earth, and over every creeping thing that creepeth upon the earth."

Dominion means *stewardship* or *control over.* Wouldn't appropriate *stewardship* be like a good baby-sitter, not a baby-sitter from a horror movie?

Wouldn't it mean respecting animals to live their own lives according to their individual natures, rather than the brutal exploitation that is not even implied by this Biblical quote? Isn't that what St. Francis did?

"Cruelty has cursed the human family for countless ages. It is impossible for one to be cruel to animals and kind to humans."

Fred A. McGrand

People often use the Bible as a weapon to get their points across. You can justify almost any point of view using the Bible if you take it literally, or we can use it as a foundation for how to live our lives.

The Bible is full of wisdom, positive proverbs, and contradictions. How can we justify Abraham giving his wife away sexually to the Pharaoh to save his own tush? And Sarah, his wife who was barren, offering Abraham her slave to have sex with, then getting jealous and beating her?

And Moses, after receiving the two tablets containing the Ten Commandments, orders the Levites to kill three thousand of their own people?

And Lot sleeping with his own daughters, and sexually offering his two daughters to aliens to save his own skin?

And Jacob lying to his father Isaac, to steal his brother's birthright? Then still qualifying to be in the genealogy to the Messiah? And Jacob's sons, so furious that their sister had been raped, kill every male in a nearby village?

Would these *family values* be accepted today?

"Cruelty must be whitewashed by a moral excuse, and a pretense of reluctance."

George Bernard Shaw

Just a few of the many rules modern society does not follow from the Old Testament Books of Leviticus and Deuteronomy are: If you bare your head or tear your garments you bring death to yourself and your community; a woman is unclean for seven days after the birth of a boy and fourteen days after the birth of a girl, so a priest has to sacrifice animals for her atonement so she can be clean; you're not allowed to wear a garment made of two different kinds of thread; not allowed to clip your hair at the temples, nor trim the edges of your beard; anyone who curses his mother or father should be put to death...So we pick and choose which Old Testament rules we adhere to.

"Men never do evil so completely and cheerfully as when they do it from a religious conviction."

Pascal
French Mathematician & Philosopher

An estimated 50% of the antibiotics manufactured in the United States are fed to animals that in turn are eaten by humans.

"...Half the world starves. What a planet. And the eating, if you're lucky enough to do any... stuffing pieces of dead animals into a hole in your face. Then munch, munch, munch."

Iris Murdoch
Author

Minks and beavers are also raised for their fur in factory farming conditions, merely for our narcissism. They are cramped into tiny wire mesh cages, often undernourished and ill.

78

"Cruelty is one fashion statement we can all do without."
Ruth McClanahan
Actress

In the wild, beavers and minks usually spend a good portion of their lives in or near water. As prisoners in factory farming, their natural instincts are suppressed, and they are made to suffer like hardened criminals on cement floors.

In the wild, minks are solitary animals, but in factory farming they are jam-packed into petite cages with other minks, causing them extreme frustration and leading to neurotic behavior, such as chewing their tails into raw meat or resorting to cannibalism.

"I feel very sorry for women who continue to purchase real fur coats. They are lacking in a woman's most important requisites, heart and sensitivity."
Jayne Meadows
Actress

The animals who are prisoners in fur farming factories, have their miserable lives extinguished by engine exhaust being pumped into their box; but sometimes the gas doesn't kill them...so some are skinned alive, contorting in pain.

"The assumption that animals are without rights and the illusion that our treatment of them has no moral significance is a positively outrageous example of Western crudity and barbarity. Universal compassion is the only guarantee of morality."
Schopenhauer
On the Basis of Morality

The larger animals raised for their fur are killed by anal electrocution. Factory fur farmers clamp the animal's lips and insert metal rods into their anus, then electrocute them.

Other methods factory fur farmers employ, to inexpensively kill animals for their fur without damaging the *goods* include, decompression chambers, neck-snapping, and poison.

"The awful wrongs and sufferings forced upon the innocent, helpless, faithful animal race, form the blackest chapter in the whole world's history."

Edward Freeman

Sheep, especially Merino sheep in Australia, are also factory farm animals. In nature, sheep have just enough wool to keep them warm. Thanks to factory farming and genetic engineering they have become wool machines. The more wrinkles, the more wool, the more money; the more misery for the sheep.

"Show me the enforced laws of a state for the prevention of cruelty to animals and I in turn will give you a correct estimate of the refinement, enlightenment, integrity and equity of that commonwealth's people."

L.T. Danshiell

In factory sheep farming, typically over half the sheep's body weight is wool, causing many sheep to die each summer from heat prostration. In the winter after being sheared, an estimated one million sheep die from freezing to death.

Another estimated ten million baby lambs die in Australia each year from neglect.

"If there is no struggle, there is no progress. Those who profess to favor freedom, and yet deprecate agitation, are people who want rain without thunder and lightning. They want the ocean without the roar of its many waters. Power concedes nothing without a demand. It never did and it never will."

Frederick Douglass
Abolitionist

Geese are also factory farm animals raised for *down,* which I loved for warmth and still own a *down* comforter I was given years ago as a gift. But I will not buy *down* now that I know the *down* feathers are *plucked* by yanking the horrified goose up in the air by his neck, tying his legs, ripping out *all* his body feathers, then tossing him back with the other geese...

The process is so barbaric veterinary surgeons who have treated the injured birds are lobbying against *live plucking* as *extremely cruel.*

"*Sentimentalist* is the abuse with which people counter the accusation that they are cruel, thereby implying that to be sentimental is worse than to be cruel, which it isn't."

Brigid Brophy

In factory geese farming, *plucking* begins at eight weeks old, and is repeated every other month for a couple of years, till they are slaughtered. A lucky goose is killed, then plucked.

"The love for all living creatures is the most noble attribute of man."

Charles Darwin

Arctic foxes are also now factory farm animals; prisoners in tiny wire mesh cages for their fur. In the wild, these foxes range from two thousand to fifteen thousand acres, they call home.

"All good things are wild, and free."

Henry David Thoreau

Photos Obtained In 1999

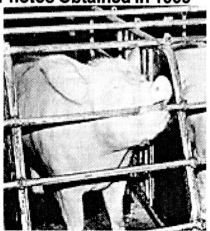

PETA INVESTIGATES BELCROSS FACTORY FARM

Photos and video documented pigs being castrated without anesthesia by holding them upside down and making incisions with a scalpel, then pulling out their testicles as they writhed in squealing pain. Pigs being reprimanded for fun by vicious blows with crowbars and pipes to their heads. A veterinarian looked the other way to all the blood, pain and abuses... Such as the sow below having her throat sliced with a scalpel, being smacked in the head with a pipe, then her throat was cut deeper as her feet twitched... A mournful moan can be heard as her throat gurgled blood, but she continued to move so the scalpel-man then sawed off her back left leg, chiding, "Give up, bitch." She gasped for air and moved her front legs, so he began sawing off her front legs as she sucked her last breath...

EATING FOR YOUR LIFE

We used our brains back in our caveman days to invent tools and weapons to overcome our physical shortcomings. Our tools and weapons allowed us to kill non-human animals, drain their blood and guts, then cook and eat their flesh.

"Nothing more strongly arouses our disgust than cannibalism, yet we make the same impression on Buddhists and vegetarians, for we feed on babies, though not our own."

Robert Louis Stevenson

Jesus too is now thought by some biblical scholars to have been a vegetarian. These biblical scholars say Jesus was a member of the Essenes, an ancient Jewish sect that were vegetarian, and stressed purity and asceticism. These scholars say the original biblical texts have been mistranslated.

The original word "food" in modern Bibles is written as "meat," and that the original word "fishweed" which is a sea-vegetable dried on the river banks by the Essenes before eating, in modern Bibles is written as the word "fish." There is other strong evidence that Jesus and his followers were vegetarian, such as he never took part in eating lamb at Passover, and kicked the animal sellers out of the temple, etc. For more information go online to www.jesusveg.com and www.jesus.com or enter "jesus vegetarian" into a search engine.

"Poor animals! How jealously they guard their pathetic bodies...that which to us is merely an evening's meal, but to them is life itself."

T. Casey Brennan

We became omnivorous by habit, but our physiology according to many physicians, is still vegetarian. Our flat teeth, configuration of our digestive systems and long intestines, bowels, constitution of our skin, saliva, stomach acids and urine are vegetarian.

When you're hungry, do you have any inborn drive to run out and kill the neighbor's dog and eat it?

"Vegetarians have lower rates of obesity, coronary heart disease, high blood pressure, large bowel disorders and gall stones," reported a recent British medical study.

The Physicians Committee for Responsible Medicine, a prestigious non-profit organization, reported that their own studies concluded the human body is of vegetarian design, like apes, our closest relatives, who are vegetarian. And that consuming meat, fish, poultry, and dairy products actually causes diseases, such as arteriosclerosis.

The British Medical Association, and finally the U.S. Government in 1996, for the first time went against the powerful meat, dairy and fish industry lobbyists, and endorsed a *vegetarian* diet for good health.

"To a man whose mind is free there is something even more intolerable in the suffering of animals than in suffering of man. For with the latter, it is at least admitted that suffering is evil and that the man who causes it is a criminal. But thousands of animals are uselessly butchered every day without a shadow of remorse.

If any man were to refer to it, he would be thought ridiculous. And that is the unpardonable crime."

Romain Rolland
Nobel Prize Author

84

Medical studies repeatedly state one of the principal risk factors for heart disease, the leading killer, is high cholesterol and saturated fats clogging the arteries from sources such as eating meat.

Human and animal cells contain cholesterol, and the Physicians Committee informs us, that our livers manufacture all the cholesterol we need. A high protein diet from eating animals can also be detrimental to our pancreas they say.

"Nothing will benefit human health and increase chances for survival of life on earth as much as the evolution to a vegetarian diet."
Albert Einstein

Despite the media propaganda by the meat industry on the dead theory that humans need some meat, repeated studies continue to find otherwise, that vegetarians are healthier than meat eaters.

"How good it is to be well-fed, healthy, and kind all at the same time."
Henry J. Heimlich

The results of many recent studies have concluded vegetarians have lower rates of angina, appendicitis, arthritis, gout, hemorrhoids and varicose veins.

"The perpetual obstacle to human advancement is custom."
John Stuart Mill
Philosopher

The average American doctor has limited or no nutritional training in medical school, and some doctors remain ignorant about nutrition their entire professional lives, according to Dr. Devananda Tandavan of the Physicians Committee for Responsible Medicine.

"If he be really serious seeking to live a good life, the first thing from which he will abstain will always be the use of animal food, because its use is simply immoral, as it involves the performance of act which is contrary to the moral feeling—killing."

Leo Tolstoy

Eating spices like ginger, which acts like a safe but slower steroid to heal joint problems are often ignored by standard medicine says Dr. Andrew Weil, a renowned doctor and author.

"The vast majority of human beings dislike and even dread all notions with which they are not familiar. Hence it comes about that at their first appearance innovators have always been derided as fools and madmen."

Aldous Huxley

Many doctors still recommend that mothers feed their children meat. "A real mistake," said Dr. Neal Barnard, President of the 4,000 member Physicians Committee For Responsible Medicine, and Director of Behavioral Studies at the Institute for Disease Prevention at George Washington University, "leading to all sorts of diseases such colic, juvenile diabetes, diarrhea and later problems such as cancer of the colon."

We are the only animal that drinks the milk of another species.

"There's is no reason to drink cows' milk at any time. It was designed for calves, it was not designed for humans, we should all stop drinking it today, this afternoon."

Dr. Frank Oski
Johns Hopkins University

It's a PR fallacy, perpetuated by the dairy industry that children need *any* dairy products to grow-up strong and healthy. Actually the opposite is true says the Physicians Committee.

"I want to pass the word to parents that cows' milk...has definite faults for some babies. It causes allergies, indigestion, and contributes to some cases of childhood diabetes."

Dr. Benjamin Spock

The American Academy of Pediatrics recommends that infants under a year should not be fed whole cows' milk. Dairy products are the leading cause of food allergies: bloating, cramps, vomiting, headaches, rashes and asthma.

An estimated 75% of Native Americans, Asian, and Mexican people, and 15% of Caucasians are lactose intolerant after 4-years-old, resulting in runny noses, bronchitis, raspy throats and perpetual ear infections.

"The unfortunate thing about this world is that good habits are so much easier to give up than bad ones."

Somerset Maugham
Author

According to the Physicians Committee, milk is suspected of causing juvenile diabetes that can lead to blindness in some children, because some children's bodies mistake the cows' milk protein as a foreign intruder and fight back by producing high levels of antibodies, but these antibodies also obliterate the cells which produce insulin in the pancreas, which they believe develops into diabetes.

"Variability is the law of life, and as no two faces are the same, so no two bodies are alike, and no two individuals react alike and behave alike under the abnormal conditions which we know as disease."

Dr. William Osler

The Physicians Committee is working arduously to change the standard basic Four Food Groups: Meat, Dairy, Fruits and Vegetables, instituted into schools and our lives by the dairy and meat

87

lobbies. The Physicians want *meat* and dairy *dropped* against the fierce protest of former Secretary of Agriculture, John R. Block, an Illinois pig farmer.

"This element (meat&dairy) of the food guides has persisted until the present time, due in part to the intensive lobbying efforts of the food industry, and despite evidence of the adverse health effects of such foods," said the Physicians Committee's report, comparing it to the tobacco industry's denial for years on the dangers of smoking.

According to the Physicians' report, the traditional Four Food Groups established in 1953 do not supply adequate nutrition. Only 9 of the 17 Recommended Daily Allowances(RDA) are being met, and that the traditional Four Food Groups' diet, contributes to *excessive fat and protein* linked to breast cancer, heart disease, obesity, kidney disease and osteoporosis.

"The old Four Food Groups serve to misinform consumers about some aspects of nutrition," said the Physicians' report. "Two of the Four Food Groups—*meat* and *dairy* products—are clearly not necessary for health and, in fact, may be detrimental to health...Populations with the lowest rates of heart disease, colon and breast cancer, and obesity consume very little meat or no meat at all."

The Physicians Committee members instrumental in designing a new Four Food Groups, included: Dr. T. Colin Campbell, Professor of Nutritional Biochemistry at Cornell University and Director of the immense China Health Project, and Dr. Oliver Alabaster, Director of the Institute for Disease Prevention at the George Washington University.

The Physicians Committee For Responsible Medicine New Four Food Groups For The 90s And Beyond

1. Whole Grains: rice, bread, pasta, hot or cold cereal, corn, millet, barley, bulgur, buckwheat groats and tortillas. The Physicians recommend building each of your meals around a hearty grain dish. Grains are rich in fiber and other complex carbohydrates, as well as proteins, B vitamins and zinc.

2. Vegetables: dark-green, leafy vegetables such as broccoli, collards, kale, mustard and turnip greens, chicory or bok choy are especially good sources of important nutrients, such as vitamin C, beta-carotene, riboflavin and other vitamins, iron, calcium and fiber. Dark yellow and orange vegetables such as carrots, winter squash, sweet potatoes and pumpkin supply further beta-carotene. The Physicians recommend generous portions and a variety of vegetables.

3. Legumes: beans, peas and lentils are excellent sources of fiber, protein, iron, calcium, zinc and B vitamins. This group also includes the daals in Indian cuisine, pulses, chickpeas, baked and refried beans, soy milk, tofu, and texturized vegetable protein.

4. Fruits: citrus fruits, melons and strawberries provide vitamin C and beta-carotene. The Physicians recommend whole fruit over fruit juices, because juices don't contain as much healthy fiber.

The Physicians also advocate a good source of vitamin B-12, such as fortified cereals and vitamin supplements.

"It is my view that the vegetarian manner of living by its purely physical effect on the human temperament would most beneficially influence the lot of mankind."

Albert Einstein

There are now many tasty and readily available foods in the supermarket that make being vegetarian much easier, such as: non-dairy, fat free, no-cholesterol, no palm or coconut oil, lactose free, faux milk; like Moca Mix and Coffee-Mate sold right alongside real milk, that are pretty good and getting better. It is definitely better for your health and the cow's life.

"The average adult can meet nutrient needs by consuming five servings of grains, three servings of legumes, three servings of vegetables and three servings of fruit each day," concluded the Physicians' report.

Morningstar Farms is one of the popular meat substitutes sold in the frozen food section of many grocery stores. They make delicious meatless breakfast links, burgers, grillers, non-bacon strips and faux chicken at this point. There are other brands that are improving all the time, and some people might like their meatless products better.

Many people think Morningstar's Grillers, Breakfast Links and non-bacon Strips actually taste better than their meat counterparts, and microwave into an appetizing meal in minutes.

Most delicous meatless products contain B-12, B-6, thiamine, calcium, and very healthy wheat and soy protein among other tasty and healthy ingredients. Of course, the ingredients and quantity supplied vary with each individual product.

Real mayonnaise is made from eggs, which are usually products of factory farming and also may be suspect to salmonella poisoning. Faux mayonnaise, vegi-dressing & spread, at this point is sold mainly in health food stores.

Eggs are used in so many products such as cookies, cake mixes, etc. that each person has to decide where to draw the line. The same is true of milk, found in ice cream, and several other products even in powder form. We can make gestures and efforts, but there's no sense driving yourself nuts.

"Most people have forgotten how to live with living creatures, with living systems, and that, in turn, is the reason why man, whenever he comes into contact with nature, threatens to kill the natural system in which and from he lives."

Konrad Lorenz
Naturalist

When vivisectors and factory farmers go the way of the slave trade and child labor, the byproducts will fall under their own weight and we won't have to worry about them.

Another meatless product sold in many grocery stores that simulates meat is Betty Crocker, Bac-os Bacon Flavor Chips, that can be added to tomato sauce and other foods for added flavoring.

A sandwich cheese alternative is cheddar flavor Smart Beat non-dairy slices, which are fat free, cholesterol and lactose free, and sold alongside regular cheese. Another delicious sandwich cheese alternative sold in many cheese flavors such as provolone etc. is appetizing Veggie Slices by Galaxy Foods, usually located in the vegetable section along with tasty Veggie Ground Round Faux Meat and Veggie Deli Slices rich in soy protein by Veggie Cusine.

A grated cheese alternative is Soyco's Grated Parmesan flavor Lite & Less, non-dairy, fat and cholesterol free, taste great.

A hot dog alternative that some think taste better than real hot dogs is Smart Dogs by Lightlife Foods, usually sold in the vegetable section and in healthfood stores. The list of tasty meat, cheese, and dairy alternatives is growing all the time.

An additional bonus for switching to meatless products is you don't have to worry about the deadly Mad-Cow disease or Ecoli bacteria attacks, many attributed to fast food meat. Although Ecoli, which comes from animal defecation, has even turned up in apple juice thought to originate from apples that fell into cattle manure because the ranchers and farmers utilized the same land, combining agri-ranching with agri-farming.

According to the Centers For Disease And Prevention, there are more than 20,000 Ecoli bacteria infections in the United States each year, attributed to meat.

"Now I can look at you in peace; I don't eat you any more."
Frank Kafka
Author

Nutritionists and progressive physicians know that plant products are great sources of protein, iron, calcium and vitamin D, because the body easily absorbs them and they don't clog up the arteries.

A recent epidemiological study, found considerable levels of cholesterol and fat in small children raised on fast foods.

"It is strange to hear people talk of humanitarianism, who are members of societies for prevention of cruelty to children and animals, and who claim to be God-loving men and women, but who, nevertheless, encourage by their patronage the killing of animals merely to gratify the cravings of appetite."
Otoman Zar

PROTEIN:

Modern society is obsessed with protein, but it is one of the easiest nutrients to obtain.

Animal protein typically comes with saturated fats which are major risk factors for heart disease. Protein from animals(milk, cheese, eggs, meat, and fish) is extremely concentrated and according to nutritionists, many people eat more than their bodies can handle.

Animal protein is linked to diabetes, gout, arthritis, osteoporosis, rheumatism, fibrositis and deficiencies in niacin, vitamin B-6, calcium, magnesium and other minerals.

"Prevention is better than a cure."

Erasmus
Scholar & Theologian

Nutritionists tell us: protein from plants are analogous with fiber which is critical for a healthy diet.

Vegetables contain abundant amounts of healthy proteins. Some of rich sources for vegetable proteins are: pasta, pulses(peas, beans and lentils) grains, nuts, peanut butter, oats, seeds, green leafy vegetables, brown rice and potatoes. A *legume* is the pod of the pea or bean that splits into two, and *pulses* are the edible seeds inside certain pods.

Nutritionists now know that if you eat a variety of plant food which is calorically adequate, it's almost impossible to be deficient in *protein*. And virtually all plants contain all the essential amino acids necessary for good health.

The false belief that people need animal protein is reportedly based on the false vivisection results obtained from rats in 1914, by Osborne and Mendel's findings on rat nutrition.

"Heaven is by favor; if it were by merit your dog would go in and you would stay out."

Mark Twain

IRON:
The average vegan(no-animal foods)diet, supplies twice the amount of iron recommended for a healthy diet.

Anemia for vegetarians is approximately the same as for meat eaters, according to the American Dietetic Association.

93

Iron deficiency, unlike protein deficiency which is almost non-existent, can be a real health concern. The same is true for consuming too much iron, usually from a supplement, can be a real health problem.

Plants that are rich in iron are: dried fruits(figs & prunes), whole grains, legumes, nuts, green leafy vegetables, seeds, nutritional yeast, pulses, molasses, and seaweed. Eating foods rich in vitamin C at the same meal helps the body absorb iron.

CALCIUM:

According to the Vegan Society, there are no reports of calcium deficiencies in vegans. They also report that studies conclude vegans and vegetarians are less at risk for osteoporosis than meat eaters, because animal protein causes the body to discharge calcium.

Rich non-animal sources of calcium are: tofu(4-times the calcium of cows' milk and a great cheese substitute in lasagna), white/wholemeal bread, taco shells, oats, soybeans, almonds, brazil nuts, pistachios, sunflower seeds, sesame seeds, flax seeds, carob, carrots, cabbage garlic, parsley, spirulina, chives, cauliflower, okra, cassava, figs, papaya, rhubarb, green leafy vegetables, dried fruit, molasses, and seaweed.

"We are born, we are given just so much food as will keep the breath in our bodies, and those of us who are capable of it are forced to work to the last atom of our strength; and the very instant that our usefulness has come to an end we are slaughtered with hideous cruelty..."

George Owell
Animal Farm

VITAMIN D

Lack of vitamin D may cause rickets(defective bone growth) especially in children. Vitamin D is produced by sunlight and can be synthesized in the skin for many months. Many nutritionists claim the vitamin D from the sun should be sufficient. Too much vitamin

D can be dangerous. You can also obtain vitamin D from non-animal sources such as margarine, soy milks, and other fortified foods.

VITAMIN A

Preformed vitamin A is not required for good health. Too much vitamin A can be dangerous.

Rich non-animal sources of vitamin A and good carotene are: green leafy vegetables, yellow fruits and vegetables.

VITAMIN B-12

The requirements for vitamin B-12 are low. It is not found in fruits or vegetables. But it is important for pregnant women and young children to have reliable sources of vitamin B-12. Reports have also suggested vitamin B-12 aids anemia and memory.

Rich non-animal sources of vitamin B-12 are: tempeh, miso (both soybean extracts), and fortified foods.

"If slaughterhouses had glass walls, everyone would be vegetarian. We feel better about ourselves and better about animals, knowing we're not contributing to their pain."
Paul & Linda McCartney

SOY:

Soy is an premium source of high quality protein. It comes from the soybean, which is the seed of the leguminous soybean plant. The soybean has been an essential element of the Chinese diet for over 4,000 years, but only used in the West for the last thirty years.

Soy has many nutritional as well as beneficial health effects. Soy contains several elements that have proven anti-carcinogenic properties, such as: protease inhibitors, phytic acid, and isoflavonoids.

The low rate of breast and colon cancer in China and Japan

is thought to be related to the large consumption of soy products in both countries.

The low percentage of menopausal symptoms in Japanese women is thought to be from soy products, which seem to mimic the dynamics of estrogen. U.S. researchers have finally confirmed in a 1996 study, "soy might relieve the miseries of the change of life."

Soy has also been shown to reduce levels of serum cholesterol, decreasing the risk for heart disease. Cholesterol in food raises the cholesterol level in your blood.

Plant products contain no cholesterol, but palm, coconut, chocolate, and hydrogenated oils do.

Meat, fish, dairy products and eggs all contain cholesterol. Chicken contains the same amount of cholesterol as beef. A four-ounce serving of chicken or beef both contain 100 milligrams of cholesterol. Lean cuts of meat contain even higher levels of cholesterol. Shellfish also contains high levels of cholesterol.

Many studies have also shown people who eat light meals or snack several times a day have lower levels of cholesterol than people who eat three big meals. Stress releases adrenaline which may also elevate cholesterol levels. Hence the beneficial effects of relaxing techniques, like meditation and massage.

Many vegetarian foods, such as: vegi-burgers, vegi-sausages and vegi-canned foods have been fortified with soy protein, which is fundamentally defatted soy flour processed and dried to form a sponge-like meat texture.

"A man can live and be healthy without killing animals for food; therefore, if he eats meat, he participates in taking animal life for the sake of his appetite. And to act so is immoral."

Leo Tolstoy

Tofu is created from coagulated soy milk. The soybeans are soaked, crushed, then heated to create soy milk. The ensuing curd is then pressed to become tofu, similar to processing cheese from dairy.

Tofu is sometimes called soy cheese and is distributed in blocks. Tofu can be whipped into a creamy texture for dips for chips or vegetables, frostings for cakes, spreads, sauces and sweet dishes, or shaped into a firm texture that can be marinated or smoked.

Tofu's drawback is its bland taste for the Western diet, so many people like to blend it into a tasty vegi-faux-meatloaf, stir-fries, soups or impart it as a supplement to other more flavorful ingredients which tofu seems to naturally absorb.

As well as being high in protein, tofu also contains calcium, and vitamins B-1, B-2 and B-3.

Tofu is sold in many grocery stores near the dairy or vegetable products or in health food stores.

Tempeh is a high protein and vitamin B-12 meatlike substance made from partially cooked fermented soybeans. It can be baked, steamed, or deep-fried as a meat substitute.

Miso is also high protein and vitamin B-12 thick fermented paste made by grinding cooked soybeans, rice or barley, and salt. Miso is used mostly for flavoring in soups, stews, casseroles and sauces.

True soysauce or shoyu is made by fermenting soybeans with roasted wheat, salt and water. Tamari is comparable but usually stronger and doesn't contain wheat. Because fermentation process takes a year, the soy sauce found in grocery stores is made by chemical hydrolsis from defatted soy flour, caramel coloring, and corn syrup.

Soymilk is a milk alternative made by soaking soybeans in water to extract fiber. It can also be made from soy flour or soy protein isolate. It has a lower fat content than milk and is sold alongside milk in most grocery stores.

Most people don't cook their own soybeans, but if you do, make sure you soak them first for a minimum of 12-hours, then drain the water, rinse them and cover them in fresh water. Bring that water to a boil, then simmer the beans for about 2-to-3-hours till they're cooked. This process is to eliminate the trypsin inhibitor which blocks the absorption of the amino acid methionine.

"We don't eat anything that has to be killed for us. We've been though a lot and we've reached a stage where we really value life."

Paul McCartney

Red kidney beans can also be dangerous and make you very sick if you eat them raw or undercooked. Soak kidney beans for approximately 8-hours in cold water.

Make sure the water covers the beans. Drain the water, rinse the beans, and put them in a pan with cold fresh water and bring to a boil.

You should boil the beans for at least 10-minutes to kill the toxin, haemaglutin, then simmer the beans for about 45-to-60-minutes till the beans have a consistent creamy grain throughout. If the core is still white and firm, the beans need more cooking.

Pressure cooking either soybeans or kidney beans is sufficient to eliminate the trypsin inhibitor in soybeans and kill the haemaglutins in kidney beans, and cuts cooking time: soybeans cook in 1-hour and kidney beans take only 10-20 minutes, but still follow the above recommended soaking and rinsing procedures for each bean.

Pulses(peas and beans) are also recommended to be soaked and boiled for about 10-minutes to kill any toxins.

WHAT IS A VEGETARIAN?

For many people *vegetarianism* becomes a religion. People are not perfect. That's why traditional religions know people will sin. But our efforts are our life. Meat was my favorite food. And Turkey was my favorite meat. Better to try and fail and get back on the path, than to make no efforts to be a better person.

A vegetarian lives on fruits, vegetables, grains, nuts, pulses and seeds. They may or may not consume dairy products and eggs(hopefully at least free-range, and that's not perfect).

A vegetarian does not eat meat, poultry, fowl, fish, crustaceans or shellfish. They also attempt to decrease and eliminate animal byproducts obtained from slaughter.

Lacto-ovo-vegetarian: Does not eat any meat or fish, but does eat dairy products and eggs.

Lacto-vegetarian: Does not eat any meat, fish, or eggs, but consumes dairy products.

Ovo-vegetarian: Does not eat any meat, fish, dairy products, but eats eggs.

Pescetarian: Does not eat any meat but eats fish, and doesn't address dairy products or eggs.

Demi-vegetarian: Eats little or no meat but may eat fish, and doesn't address dairy products or eggs.

Vegan: Does not eat or use any animal product or by-product such as leather, some soaps, animal fats, or gelatin which is made from boiled animal bones, tendons and skin. Gelatin is used to make Jell-O and other desserts. Vegans use Agar-Agar which is a gelatin substitute obtained from seaweed and the root of the Kuzu.

Fruitarian: Does not eat any meat, fish, or plant food that has to be harvested by killing the plant, and hardly consumes any processed or cooked foods. Other vegetarians believe that because plants don't have a central nervous system they don't experience pain as we know it. Fruitarians live mostly on fruits, grains and nuts.

Macrobiotic: A diet maintained for spiritual reasons, that consist of ten levels of achievement. Food is deemed negative (yang) or positive(yin). All animal products are considered negative. The lower levels are not vegetarian. As a person moves to higher levels, animal products are gradually eliminated. The highest level excludes fruits and vegetables, and the elite exist on brown rice.

"Life is *life's* greatest gift. Guard the life of another creature as you would your own because it is your own. On life's scale of values, the smallest is no less precious to the creature who owns it than the largest."

Lloyd Biggle Jr.

WHY BECOME A VEGETARIAN?

Cruelty (the suffering and pain of the animals) is the number one reason most people become vegetarian, according to a recent study.

Health is the second most frequent reason cited for becoming a vegetarian. Meat, dairy and egg consumption are linked to heart disease, high blood pressure, cancer, obesity, diet-related diabetes, and a hosts of other health problems.

A low fat, high fiber vegetarian diet along with exercise, no smoking, and stress reduction programs was the best way to good health and proven to reverse heart disease, as documented in the book: "Dr. Dean Ornish's Program for Reversing Heart Disease."

Fiber is not found in any animal products. Soluble fiber aids in retarding the absorption of cholesterol and reduces the amount of cholesterol your liver has to manufacture. Good sources of fiber are: beans, oats, barley and some fruits and vegetables.

According to studies by the American Dietetic Association, vegetarians have lower mortality rates from coronary artery disease, chronic degenerative diseases, and lower rates of hypertension, Type II diabetes, lung cancer, obesity, osteoporosis, kidney stones, gall-stones and diverticular disease.

Studies have also shown people who adopted a vegetarian diet reduced their fat intake by 26% and had their cholesterol levels drop significantly in just six weeks.

The Environment is the third reason cited for becoming a vegetarian. Protecting the destruction of the rain forests to make room for lucrative cattle ranching, and the overgrazing of vast lands being ravished.

Remember, becoming a vegetarian is a gradual process. Check with a nutritionist, or your doctor should you be under care, before making dietary changes that may affect your particular health needs.

"It was a bad place when you came, and it will be a bad place when you leave. Lighting-up your own little world, is enough for one lifetime."

Joseph Campbell
Philosopher & Mythologist

101

A FEW FAMOUS VEGETARIANS:

Entertainers: Richard Gere, Steven Seagal, Christie Brinkley, Leonardo DiCaprio, Leonard Nimoy, Paul Newman, Scott Adams (*Dilbert* Cartoonist), Bob Dylan, John Denver, Tina Turner, Alicia Silverstone, k.d. Lang, Dennis Weaver, Mary Tyler Moore, George Harrison, Kim Basinger, Cloris Leachman, Berke Breathed(*Bloom County* Cartoonist), Melissa Etheridge, Linda and Paul McCartney, John Cleese, Madonna, Butterfly McQueen(*"Prissy" Gone With The Wind*), James Cromwell (Star -*Babe & LA Confidential)*, Elvira, Sara Hickman(Singer), Ingrid Newkirk, Cleveland Amory(Author of Christmas Cat & Founder of The Fund for Animals), Paul Harvey Jr., Rue McClanahan(Actress), Alice Walker(Author of *The Color Purple*), Ted Kirkpatrick(Hardrocker), Dr. Neal Barnard(Author of *The Power of Your Plate*), Bruce Hornsby(Musician), Eric Johnson(Rock Guitarist), Angie Dickinson, Peggy McCay(Actress-*Days of Our Lives*), Kevin Nealon (Comedian *Saturday Night Live),* Kathleen Madigan(Comedian) and Grace Slick(Rock Singer), and jazz great Herbie Hancock.

Historical: Benjamin Franklin, St. Francis, Gandhi, Albert Einstein, Socrates, Plato, Aldous Huxley, St. John Chrysostom, Isaac Bashevis Singer, Leonardo da Vinci, Leo Tolstoy, Sir Isaac Newton, H.G. Wells, Upton Sinclair, Mark Twain, Robert Louis Stevenson, Dr. Albert Schweitzer, Henry David Thoreau, Ralph Waldo Emerson, George Orwell, Frank Kafka, Charles Darwin, and George Bernard Shaw...amongst a few.

Sports Personalites: Tony La Russa(Coach-St.Louis Cardinals), Orlando Cepeda(Hall of Fame Baseball Player), Peter Burwash(Tennis Player), Chip Oliver, Marv Levy(Coach-Buffalo Bills), Dave Scott(Five Time Iron Man Triathlon), Murray Rose(Olympic Swimming Legend), Willie Davis(Former LA Dodgers' Outfielder), Dr. Ruth Heidrich(Iron Woman Triathlete), and Dr. David Ryde(15-Years, Medical Advisor for British Olympians).

TAX DOLLARS FOR KILLING

HUNTING

"The real cure for our environmental problems is to understand that our job is to salvage Mother Nature...We are facing a formidable enemy in this field.

It is the *hunters*...and to convince them to leave their guns on the wall is going to be very difficult."

Jacques Cousteau
Oceanographer

Approximately 93% of the population doesn't hunt states the Manual For Animal Rights. Your tax dollars support the tiny 7% of the population who do hunt. Hunting license fees cover only about 10% of the cost of the programs, service, and federal management. The US Fish and Wildlife programs are subsidized hundreds of millions each year, up to 90% of their revenue, from your tax dollars.

The following excerpts were written in by a former hunter, and are used with permission from Animal Rights Online. "I hunted for 30 years. For various reasons, mostly because my father did, and my grandfather did."

"The time will come when men such as I look upon murder of animals as they now look on the murder of men."

Leonardo Da Vinci

On the state level follow the money trail, then you'll see why politicians cater to the small hunting population. In addition to the revenue from state hunting licenses which do cover a large amount of the state's cost, the amount of money each state receives from the federal government's excise tax on guns and ammunition, depends on the number of licensed hunters in that state.

A hunter's confession continues: "I guess I hunted because I did. At first, killing was thrilling, then anti-climatic, then distasteful. Then you begin to wonder why you are doing it."

"Of all the creatures ever made he(man)is the most detestable...He is the only creature that inflicts pain for sport, knowing it to be pain."

Mark Twain

That's why state politicians often set up programs to please hunters, to get those federal dollars...State game officials are appointed, not elected, and are paid from the hunting revenues.

A hunter's confession continues: "After pursuing elk for 7-years in the Bob Marshall Wilderness, I got an easy shot at a 6-point bull and passed. If he could elude me for that long, what business did I have to kill him and hang his head where people who had never experienced his world could look at him...not in his magnificence, but in an artificially posed mount...Who would be better off had I ended the animal's life?"

"Since a large portion of the funds which run the department and pay the salaries are from hunters and fishermen, there is a strong tendency for the agency to consider itself not as representing and working for the general public but that they need only serve their financial sponsors--the hunters and fishermen of the state.
If your financial support is dependent on the activity of hunting, obviously very few are going to question the ecological or ethical problems with it.

104

Many would argue that these funding arrangements constitute a prostitution of the public lands for the benefit of the few."

David Favre
Professor of Wildlife Law

Hunters often say they are performing a service, killing animals that would otherwise over populate and starve to death. Their stock quip is: "A quick bullet is better than slowly starving to death."

But it's estimated that for every animal killed by a hunter, two scramble away gravely wounded. Imagine if governments around the world systematically gunned-down overcrowded populations under the specious argument they were preventing starving.

A hunter's confession continues: "I began to look at hunting differently. It certainly isn't needed by anyone or anything...most animals are not hunted, and do just fine. Hunters continually harp on deer overpopulation...In November 1989, I was shot by a deer hunter, while on my own property."

"We have never understood why men mount the heads of animals and hang them up to look down on their conquerors. Possibly it feels good to these men to feel superior to animals, but does it not seem that if they were sure of it they would not have to prove it? Often a man who is afraid must constantly demonstrate his courage and, in the case of the hunter, must keep a tangible record of his courage."

John Steinbeck
Nobel Prize Author

If hunters were attempting to perform a benevolent service they would hunt only sick and old animals. Or to a lesser extent the females or starving young of the species, but that is not the case.

The aim of most hunters is to kill the biggest and strongest male in his prime either to showoff as a display, trophy potential, or for the abundant meat; or combination of all three.

A hunter's confession continues: "The irresponsible hunter left me for dead...my twelve-year-old son loaded me in a truck and drove me 40 miles to a hospital. That didn't dampen my enthusiasm though, and is not the reason I quit, but it did give me a solid taste of what the animals endure."

"When a man wants to murder a tiger, it's called a sport; when a tiger wants to murder him it's called ferocity."

George Bernard Shaw

Animals did fine for thousands of years on their own without having to be killed to prevent overpopulation. In most cases in the wild, animals only propagate to the limit the environment can sustain them.

A hunter's confession continues: "I guess I began to understand that the animal I was looking at through a scope was not just a target, but a living thing. A thing that suffered when shot, a thing that I had no right to kill, though I had the privilege to do so, by virtue of paying another person a fee for a license. Think about that."

"The average beast of prey is a decent creature who merely kills for the sake of food or in a fight against an enemy. It is only man who calls killing sport and kills for the pleasure of killing; not for food, not for self-defense, but just to satisfy some primitive instinct, once necessary and now perverted."

Gilbert Murray
Author/Linguist

A hunter's confession continues: "The animal is minding his own business when you go into a store, pay a fee and walk out with a license to kill the animal, what a deal. I shot my last animal that will ever fall to my gun in November 1992. I hunted until January 1997."

Conservationists argue, game management programs operate under the guise of population control, but their policies are designed to actually increase animal populations so hunters will have a bounty of animals to kill.

"The American public is FOOTING THE BILL for predator-control programs that cause the systematic slaughter of refuge animals. Raccoons and red fox, squirrel and skunks are but a few of the many egg-eating predators trapped and destroyed in the name of wildlife management programs.

Seagulls are shot, fox pups poisoned, and coyotes killed by aerial gunners in low flying aircraft. This wholesale destruction is taking place on the only federal lands set aside to protect America's wildlife!"

Humane Society of The United States

Wildlife management purports that their goal is to control animal populations to prevent starving. Yet their practices are quite the opposite, such as the New York Department of Environmental Conservation acquiring pheasants raised in captivity specifically to be released in hunting areas to be shot down. Your tax dollars at work.

A hunter's confession continues: "In five years, I discovered I could love the outdoors and its experiences, which I still dearly enjoy, without killing. The guns stay at home when I take to the field now...I have turned more to shooting competition for satisfaction and achievement."

"Wild animals never hunt for the sport. Man is the only one to whom the torture and death of his fellow creatures is amusing in itself."

James Anthony Froude
English Historian

Statistics indicate that hunters also inadvertently kill hundreds of people each year. In Vermont, dairy farmers routinely drape bull's-eyes on their cows so hunters won't shoot them by mistake. And kids are dressed in bright neon colors, so they won't be accidentally shot by hunters.

A hunter's confession continues: "Is hunting worse than factory farming? No. Does that make hunting right? No. Am I responsible for the death of animals, even though I am a vegetarian, don't use leather or fur? Sure. One only need observe the bugs on my truck's grill to see that. But I have decided to minimize my impact on animals and work to help them, rather than kill them. I have a lot of making up to do."

Gary Wapiti
Former Hunter

"The creed of maximum sustainable yield unmasks the (wildlife management) rhetoric about humane service to animals. It must be a perverse distortion of the ideal of humane service to accept or engage in practices, the explicitly goal of which is to insure that there will be a larger, rather than smaller, number of animals to kill! With humane friends like that, wild animals certainly do not need any enemies."

Tom Regan
Philosopher & Animal Rights Activist

Culling is process of killing animals that have become pests or are damaging the environment in some way. Typically, animals that are deemed pests or have overpopulated is usually because man has interfered along the way. Ironically, man is by far the biggest pest and has done the utmost damage to the environment.

Wildlife management and farmers are two of the worst culprits of culling. Wildlife management's typical response is to organize a hunt...historically, hunting is analogous with bringing animals near or into extinction, like the buffalo and passenger pigeon.

108

"It is an unfortunate fact that those people who are most eloquent in their demand for the conservation of animals are often those most eager to violate animal life at the first opportunity."
Reverend Andrew Linzey
Christian Argument For Vegetarianism

Farmers are always arguing they must cull animals that have overpopulated because they thrive on a certain crop, or were introduced for some other manmade scheme, like to control some other pest, that more often than not backfires.

Conservationists assert that man usually creates the animal overpopulation problem, so we should be able to undo our mess without massive killing. Modern techno-farmland by its very essence is an ecosystem out of sync.

"For thousands of years, peoples all over the world have used farming methods based on natural ecosystems where potential pest populations are self-regulating. These ideas are now being explored in organic farming and permaculture."
David Cowles
English Author & Animal Rights Activist

Hunters and others proclaim that hunting is a natural drive. If this was true, wouldn't we all be compelled to hunt our neighbors' pets? And even if hunting is a leftover drive in the genes, or passed down genetically, or if it was developed from observation, it is no longer needed. There were even people thousands of years ago who didn't eat meat. Isn't so-called civilized man suppose to control impulses?

"Hunting...the least honorable form of war on the weak."
Paul Richard

As St. Paul said, "When I was a child...I thought as a child..."As a kid I bought a BBgun with my newspaper route money, and shot cans and bottles at first. One day a bird landed in a nearby tree. I aimed and shot...So I know the sudden rush of the hunt...it's the end result, killing or wounding another life that like myself had no choice being born. I can't remember if I hit the bird or not; memory is a faulty faculty-- I have two distinct versions of the same incident: in one version I hit the bird and feel terrible, and in the other he flies off... but that was the end of my hunting career.

My urge to shoot was contradicted by the paradox of the end result: I didn't want to kill that little bird, who was just trying to live like the rest of us. We live in a dimension of pairs of opposites always operating simultaneously, and for most humans, hunting is unnecessary.

"The very people who shudder most over the cruelty of the hunter are apt to forget that slaughter, in the grimmest sense of the word, is a process they entrust daily to the butcher and that unlike the game of the forests, even the dumbest creatures in the slaughter-house knows what lies in store for them."

Lewis Mumford
Author

Fighter pilots often speak of the adrenaline rush they feel rocketing across the sky...before launching missiles at a target...It's like a video game. They get the high without the downside, without witnessing the destruction they are causing. They miss the end result... the horror of killing and maiming thousands... but to the pilot it's antiseptic. Sometimes the reality catches up with them later...I worked for over two years in a psychiatric hospital that admitted veterans who had seen action...if there was any thrill, it was gone.

"I could not have slept tonight if I had left that helpless little creature to perish on the ground," said President Abraham Lincoln to a disgruntled aid he had angered, by stopping to put a fledgling back in its nest.

Psychiatrists tell us, survival is the strongest drive. So if we all followed that impulse, every time we're hungry we would run into the grocery store whether we had money or not, and snatch what we wanted.

"I do not regard flesh-food as necessary for us at any stage and under any clime in which it is possible for human beings ordinarily to live. I hold flesh-food to be unsuited to our species."
Gandhi

Sex is the second strongest drive, say psychiatrists. If people responded to that instinct, there would be infinite sexual assaults. Anarchy would be the norm, if the majority acted on impulses.

"I do not believe that, even when we fulfill our minimum obligations not to cause pain, we have the right to kill animals. I know I would not have a right to kill you, however painless, just because I liked your flavor, and I'm not in a position to judge that your life is worth more to you than the animal's to it."
Brigid Brophy

Competitive sports are surely a more acceptable outlet for man's aggressive urges, than intentionally killing docile deer, rabbits, fowl, or even baiting bear then shooting them. We just happen to be the species on the top of the evolutionary ladder...with an exaggerated opinion of ourselves.

"The squirrel you kill in jest, dies in earnest."
Henry David Thoreau

But if we insist on hunting, why not let hunters form a league of different teams and use rubber bullets to hunt each other? Maybe they could be sponsored by advertisers and awarded cash and prizes. Let them experience the thrill of the hunt and the terror and pain of being hunted...

111

"Hunting is barbaric, unless the animals could shoot back..."
Bernie Ward
Radio Commentator

Gandhi goes farther: "Possession of arms implies an element of fear, if not cowardice."

FISHING

I was an avid fisherboy. The only opening day of fishing season I ever missed, was because I needed an operation. Yet before being operated on and later that evening...I was still daydreaming about the thrill of opening day.

"When a man wantonly destroys one of the works of man, we call him a vandal. When he wantonly destroys one of the works of God, we call him a sportsman."
Joseph Wood Krutch
Educator/Naturalist

I continued fishing right up to my early 30s, behind a wall of delusion that fish couldn't feel pain, and I didn't want to think about it and ruin my fun. I loved the camaraderie, camping, and solitude more than the actual fishing.

"The three prerequisites for angling: a hook, a line, and a stinker."
John Bryant

The Medway Report, a three year investigation by scientists and representatives from shooting and angling organizations, concluded that fish do feel pain and suffering through their complex nervous systems and sensory organs.

The Medway Report detailed the death imposed by fishing is a gradual asphyxiation, and that the barbed hook snagged in the head caused extreme pain...because we now know the brain of the fish contains endogenous opiates and receptors capable of sensing pain,

112

the same as humans and other vertebrates.

"It was like hunting fish with an underwater gun, a sport he had been foolish enough to try. At one moment there is a fish—graceful, mysterious, desirable and free—and the next moment there is nothing but struggling and blood and confusion."

Iris Murdoch
Irish Author

As I fished less and less, I gradually accepted fish are not dumb, as if intelligence makes it acceptable to kill a sentient being...Fish just operate on different software. They are extremely adept in their own world and even outsmart many fishermen. And fishing for many humans, is very unnecessary.

"A fine morning's killing, ay! All their necks wrung—all dead birds! Once they could fly—fly and swim! Fly and swim! All dead now..."

Marie Corelli

Behavioral studies have determined that fish have complex forms of learning such as operant conditioning, serial reversal, probability and avoidance learning abilities.

"The art of angling, the cruelest, the coldest, and the stupidest of pretended sports."

Lord Byron

The first step giving-up fishing, is sometimes throwing the fish back after you catch him. I remember thinking how wonderful I was, when I graduated to that level of consciousness...

"There is no sport in the world like mountaineering, its pleasures are not marred by the slaughter of innocent animal life, nor discomfiture to any of our fellow-beings."

George D. Abraham

Nutritionists say the health benefits from eating fish, if you could find any waters not polluted, can be obtained from a vegetarian diet.

"What with our hooks, snares, nets, and dogs we are at war with all living creatures, and nothing comes amiss but that which is either too cheap or too common; and all this is to gratify a fantastical palate."

Senaca (5BC-65AD)

I finally became conscious that being yanked by a hook for thirty yards as I got my yucks, was still painful for the fish and leaves a lesion open to infection. Then handling the fish to get the hook out, rubs off their disease-fighting coating that covers their scales...

"No doubt Jack the Ripper excused himself on the grounds that it was human nature."

A.A. Milne
English Author

Maybe it's time to stop letting ourselves off the hook. We're not going to change the world. But our efforts are our lives.

"All beings tremble before danger and death."

Buddha

THRILLS AND SIDESHOWS

RODEOS

"The rodeo folks send their animals to the packing houses, where I have seen cattle so extensively bruised that the only areas in which the skin was attached was the head, neck, legs and belly.

I have seen animals with six to eight ribs broken from the spine, and at times puncturing the lungs. I have seen as much as two and three gallons of free blood accumulated under the detached skin."

Dr. C.G. Haber
Veterinarian & USDA Meat Inspector For Three Decades

No one can deny the adrenaline-rush a conflict like rodeo or bull fighting might produce. But why must our fun and money-making be at the expense of the fear and pain of living animals? Why must we amuse ourselves by inflicting pain on others, like we did almost 2,000 years ago at the Roman Coliseum, throwing Christians out into the arena for the lions to chase down and rip apart? Thousands of years have past, but we still blindly lust after the pain of others for our entertainment? Yet technologically we've advanced to space travel...And surely video games offer a similar thrill and rush, without inflicting pain, suffering, and death on living beings...

"Any religion or philosophy which is not based on a respect for life is not a true religion or philosophy."

Dr. Albert Schweitzer

115

The mechanical-bucking-bull is the sport in many cowboy bars. I'm sure we can produce a life-like mechanical-bucking-bull, bronco, calf and steer, should the market be there. The sexy cowboys or cowgirls would still need the talent and the audiences would still be entertained.

For additional stimulation, wagering should be allowed. Faux rodeos would probably make a lot more money and draw huge crowds. The public would be satisfied--and, with nobody taunting him, so would Mr. Bull.

"I don't think you should hurt or kill animals just to entertain an audience. Animals should have some rights. There are a lot of directors...who will injure animals to further a plot. I will have none of it."

James Mason

We no longer have the excuses, nor can we claim ignorance like many of our forefathers who were unaware of the intellect, awareness, emotions, and social requirements of animals.

"...This rage— I have never forgotten it—contained every anger, every revolt I had ever felt in my life—the way I felt when I saw the black dog hunted, the way I felt when I watched old Uncle Henry taken away...the way I felt whenever I had seen people or animals hurt for the pleasure or profit of others."

Ellen Glasgow
American Novelist

The American rodeo audiences, see only seconds of the animal's distressing exhibition: such as a bucking bronco or bull, roping or steer wrestling. But to get to this point there are thousands of misery hours in unconsenting practice sessions, continuous travel, and according to the Animal Rights Manual, inappropriate ventilation and less than stellar care, including lack of food, water, and rough handling.

116

"Every civilizing step in history has been ridiculed as sentimental, impractical, or womanish, etc., by those whose fun, profit, or convenience was at stake."

J. Gilbert
Actor

The Manual of Animal Rights reported that 50% of the rodeo rider's score is calculated by the performance of the bucking horse or bull, so riders are spurred to provoke a frenzied ride by yanking on a bucking strap that vice-grips the animal's thighs and groin.

They also reported that electric prods and raking spurs are used on the animals to incite ferocious conduct. Rodeo animals routinely incur injuries such as: bruises, broken bones, paralysis, severed tracheas and even death.

"Who can go to a rodeo and then criticize the hunter? An expertly placed bullet would be the best gift a rodeo horse could receive."

Roger Caras

The macho practice of smashing rodeo animals to the ground, has led to internal organs bursting and slow excruciating deaths.

"All nature protests against the barbarity of man, who misapprehends, who humiliates, who tortures his inferior brethren."

Jules Michelet
French Historian

Veterinarians who treat rodeo animals have also reported calves having their spinal cords severed from by being lassoed at 20 mph.

"Never doubt that a small group of thoughtful, committed citizens can change the world; indeed, it is the only thing that ever does."

Margaret Mead
Anthropologist

CIRCUSES

"When you see chimps all dressed up at the circus, what you don't see is the training: the chimps being clunked in the head with a metal bar."

Jane Goodall
World Renowned Primatologist

In circuses, unlike rodeos, the pain and suffering of the animals goes on behind the scenes, before and after the performances. Some circuses have now dropped animal acts, proving our entertainment doesn't have to come at the expense of animals.

"Despite one or two minority appeals our society is not outraged at man's unremitting use of the animal world. Ecologists and environmentalists may talk of ecological consciousness or environmental responsibility but seldom, if ever, is this responsibility articulated towards other non-human species in particular."

Reverend Andrew Linzey

Circus animals are hauled thousands of miles annually through all types of weather in unclimated, crowded railroad cars or beast wagons—trailer trucks with bars on one side. The large animals like the elephants, are chained in squalid conditions, and the non-pack animals like solitary tigers, are cramped into cages and compelled to live in packs.

"Wild animals are not meant to be owned, any more than human beings are. Nobody has the right to pass a cougar or a gorilla on from hand to hand."

Pat Derby
Former Animal Trainer; Founder of *Paws*

Circus animals are typically wild animals trained to perform by reward and punishment systems, such as withholding food.

Electric goads, whips, sticks and gun shots are some of the methods used to force the animals to execute aberrant acts, such as making a bear dance, or an elephant teeter on small buckets or reel-up on its hind legs, or a lion jump through a hoop on fire.

"Suppose that tomorrow a group of beings from another planet were to land on earth, beings who considered themselves as superior to you as you feel yourself to be to other animals. Would they have the right to treat you as you treat the animals..."

John Harris
Writer

Most circus animals endure continuous psychological and physical pain. Similar to zoo animals, circus animals display neurotic behavior, such as apathy, pacing, and rocking like humans you would see in a psychiatric hospital suffering mental distress.

The typical physical ailments circus animals suffer include shackle ulcers, herpes, kidney and liver disease.

"As we increasingly become aware of the One Life breathing in each brother form of life, we learn the meaning of compassion(to be born again), which literally means to suffer with...How does the self cause the desire which causes suffering?...by the illusion of separateness, the unawareness of One."

Christmas Humphreys
Author

In our evolutionary process of consciousness awakening, we are always abandoning formerly acceptable or at least tolerated customs and traditions, such as tar-and-feathering, racism and sexism. The time has long since come, for us to realize animals have a right to their own lives and it's wrong to abuse them for our entertainment.

"My prayer is that we have gone through wars, and the world someday will be startled into some new realization of the sanctity of life, animal and human."

Christoper Morley

ZOOS

Follow the money. On the news recently another prestigious zoo was caught selling their exotic animals to private *fenced ranches* to be *hunted* year round for $300. to $2000. Wounding an animal cost the same. The newscaster remarked this was a common, little known policy for zoos to raise extra revenue.

"Man must get his thoughts, words and actions out of this vast moral jungle. We are not predators. We are, hopefully, more than instinctive killers and selfish brutes."

H. Jay Dinsah

I loved zoos as a kid, till I realized in my 20s that zoos are just animal prisons under the guise of education or saving endangered species.

"You have to love animals for what they are or leave them alone. The best thing you can do if you love them is leave them alone and see that other people do too."

Pat Derby

To continue funding, zoos are continuously paying themselves PR lip-service as saviors of endangered species.

But according to the UK Manual of Animal Rights, approximately 6,000 species of mammal, bird, reptile, amphibian, fish and invertebrate are endangered, along with 578 species catalogued as borderline. An estimated 50 to 100 animal and plant species becomes extinct daily because poaching, pollution, and humans continue to destroy their natural habitats for profit.

Only a minuscule number of species have been so-called saved by posh captive breeding programs. These programs are the PR fodder for the media.

"When someone says they're going to save me, I run for my life."

Henry David Thoreau

120

Like zoos, society could also save the homeless by snagging them into captivity, then feeding them and offering medical attention. Like the captured zoo animals, they might live longer than out in the streets. But every so often, a few would feel the drive for freedom, choosing quality over quantity, and attempt to scale the fake mountains and barriers, and that would be even more crowd-pleasing--I mean educational.

"All zoos actually offer the public, in return for the taxes spent upon them, is a form of idle witless amusement, compared to which a visit to the state penitentiary, or even a state legislature in session, is informing, stimulating and ennobling."

H.L. Mencken
American Editor & Critic

Zoo animals, similar to circus animals, and human prisoners exhibit the same neurotic demeanor of wide-spectrum stress-induced frustration: pacing, obsessive grooming, anger-apathy oscillation, head-banging, depression and self-mutilation.

"We would consider it cruel to confine a dog permanently in a kennel. Yet we visit zoos where hundreds of wild animals are kept permanently in the equivalent of a kennel. It is as if we, like the animals, become trapped within the zoo concept and we cannot see beyond the bars. We forget that wildlife in zoos is still wildlife."

Virginia McKenna
Beyond The Bars

The animals' natural habitats may also have their own stressful conditions, but like the homeless man desperately trying to escape his comfortable surroundings, there's nothing like freedom, nothing like being in your own natural habitat. Nothing like being where you belong, rather than being controlled under somebody's beck-and-call.

"The zoo is a prison for animals who have been sentenced without trial and I feel guilty because I do nothing about it. I wanted to see an oyster-catcher, so I was no better than the people who caged the oyster-catcher for me."

Russell Hoban
World Renowned Children's Author

Many species don't adapt well in zoos such as: pandas, marine animals, and several species of birds, etc., but that doesn't stop the zoos. They go for the star-studded animals that will attract the largest crowds to bring in the most money.

"We cannot glimpse the essential life of a caged animal, only the shadow of its former beauty."

Julia Allen Field

A typical zoo story: Knight-Ridder Newspapers reported Kijana, an 11-month old baby African elephant died in a Zoo from a bacteria infection, possibly from stress and a weakened immune system, that lacked his mother's milk.

Elephants hate zoos so much, he was the first elephant born in captivity since 1984.

Being born in captivity is so unnatural, his mother rejected him at birth and he had to be bottle-fed.

The zoo's answer: "A goat named Rafiki was placed in Kijana's pen to keep him company...," the article proudly stated.

But the important thing: "Visitors came in droves to see the new addition..." said the article about his money-drawing power. "African elephants in the wild learn to parent from each other. In captivity, the chance for a female rejecting her baby is much higher..."

122

"We wanted to go to the baby zoo, and the elephant was one of the things I wanted them(her children) to see," said a visitor. "I was very upset." (Because she made the trip for nothing, not that the baby elephant, Kijana, had died).

Wouldn't a video of wild elephants and their babies in their natural environment be more educational and true? Rather than the poor neurotic zoo animals.

According to this article, the zoo spent $125,000 in care and food on Kijana, but the misery index is unmeasurable.

So in the kindness area, what did zoo officials learn? Nothing: They were exuberant to learn Kijana's "mother, Lisa, may be pregnant again..."

"What is so beneficial to the people as liberty, which we see not only to be greedily sought after by men, but also by beast, and to be preferred to all things."

Cicero(106-43 B.C.)

Zoos proclaim they have three major missions: keeping the money coming in, education, and saving endangered species.

Their educational defense is: most people would never see these animals in person. Too bad.

Most folks will never see an Eskimo in person or a pygmy, but we don't pay poachers to capture them and stick them in cages or in limited, simulated environments. Though some people might if they could fool the public and pull it off as educational.

The best way to learn about an animal is to study the animal in its natural environment without interfering, like Charles Darwin and Jane Goodall. The second best might be videos, public TV programs, and magazines like National Geographic.

"Moral education, as I understand it, is not about inculcating obedience to law or cultivating self-virtue, it is rather about finding within us an ever-increasing sense of the worth of creation. It is about how we can develop and deepen our intuitive sense of beauty and creativity." Reverend Andrew Linzey

Zoos often claim they are only sustaining endangered animal species until their habitats are safe for them to be returned. Sort of like infinite holding-stations... If this wasn't so sad, it's almost laughable.

After being imprisoned in zoos, fed and imprinted by humans, these poor, neurotic animals could probably never survive in the wild. In captivity, like prisoners of war, they have lost their identities: how to fly, build dens, hunt, and teaching their young...the ultimate traumatic-stress-syndrome.

"If an animal does something we call it instinct; if we do the same thing for the same reason, we call it intelligence."
Will Cuppy
American Author & Humorist

If zoologists really wanted to protect endangered species they would be environmentalists, working to restore the polluted natural habitats of endangered animals and working to protect endangered species from poachers (some sell to zoos), hunters, pollution, and humans destroying the animals' natural habitats.

"Human liberation will begin when we understand that our evolution and fulfillment are contingent on the recognition of animal rights and on a compassionate and responsible stewardship of nature."
Dr. Michael W. Fox

Food For Thought Zoo Stories: *Female Gorilla Rescues Toddler After He Fell Into A Zoo Exhibit*, proclaimed an Associated Press Article.

124

"Brookfield, Ill.—A toddler fell into a gorilla exhibit at the Brookfield Zoo on Friday afternoon, and was rescued by a female gorilla who cradled the child and brought him to zookeepers."

ABC News reported, that the Paris Zoo announced the death of a female gorilla, who refused to eat for one month after her mate of 34-years suddenly died.

HORSE AND DOG RACING

Money is the name of the game. There is no pretense to hide behind.

In my 20s I went to dog and horse racing tracks. I enjoyed the rush of gambling, with zero awareness of the animals' side of the equation. I just assumed animals worth this much money, must be treated royally.

"True human goodness, in all its purity and freedom, can come only to the fore when its recipient has no power. Mankind's true moral test, its fundamental test(which lies deeply buried from view), consists of its attitude towards those who are at its mercy: animals. And in this respect mankind has suffered a fundamental debacle, a debacle so fundamental that all others stem from it."

Milan Kundera
Prolific Czech Poet, Playwright, Novelists
The Unbearable Lightness of Being

An Australian study reported in the UK Manual of Animal Rights, found that 42% of race horses suffered from a disease called pulmonary hemorrhage (EIPH), blood in their lungs and windpipes, from extreme exercising. From over rigorous training, all race horses all predisposed to pulmonary hemorrhage disease.

"The worst sin towards our fellow creatures in not to hate them, but to be indifferent to them, that's the essence of inhumanity."

George Bernard Shaw

If you've ever been fortunate to be near bareback horses when the sun is setting, you know horses relish a good gallop. They will take off and canter till their hearts are content. Greyhound dogs also enjoy a good romp.

And some people enjoy a good exercise workout. But few people enjoy being forced to workout, similar to the rigors of military basic training— But most people choose to go into the armed services, race horses and greyhounds are always unconsenting. We steal their lives and pervert what was a pleasurable drive into a grueling life.

"Once we admit that we have the right to inflict unnecessary suffering, you destroy the very basis for human society."

John Galsworthy
English Author

Many race horses and greyhound racing dogs commonly endure painful lameness, fractures, joint sprains, and ripped ligaments.

Steeplechasing, according to the UK Animal Rights Manual, by its very layout, is calculated so that the horses suddenly drop after jumping and many have broken their necks, legs, etc. or suffer life-long injuries.

"Cruelty to animals is one of the distinguishing vices of low and base minds. Wherever it is found, it is a certain mark of ignorance and meanness, a mark which all the external advantages of wealth, splendor, and nobility, cannot obliterate. It is consistent neither with learning nor true civility."

William Jones

Doping painful injuries to keep the animals racing is not uncommon, according to the Manual of Animal Rights, as well as administering undetectable, performance-enhancement drugs, electrical stimuli, and whips... Even though some of these practices and others such as dog-blooding are illegal, the enticement for thousands or even millions of dollars is just too great a temptation. That's what the Our Father Prayer is all about: "Lead us not into temptation..."

"There is something in animals beside the power of motion. They are not machines; they feel."
Charles De Secondat Montesquieu
French Philosopher

Most racing animals reportedly are housed in the barest living quarters, except for a few of the top money makers.

In the dead of winter on the East Coast a few years back, hundreds of racing greyhounds perished in a suspicious fire in an unheated warehouse. Firefighters were shocked these million-dollar-babies were living in dismal, frigid conditions.

"Much of the indifference, apathy, and even cruelty we see has its origin in the false education given the young concerning the rights of animals, and their duty toward them."
J. Tod Ferrier

On a positive baby step, Paul Harvey's radio commentary complimented Lucy Reum, former Chairperson of the Illinois State Racing Board and the first woman ever elected to the National Association of State Racing Commissioners not only for initiating improvements to the living conditions of the migratory grooms, hot-walkers, and exercise-riders and their families, but also for setting up instructional classrooms to train these handlers how to properly care for the horses.

If the direct caregivers are treated with more dignity, maybe they in turn will treat the horses more compassionately.

She has also launched a renovation program that replaced many of the old wooden barns with modern concrete barns equipped with sprinklers to prevent the too often horrible fires.

Photo Obtained in 1999

Somber Circus Bear Between Shows

THE TRUTH ABOUT TOXOPLASMOSIS

The main cause of toxoplasmosis, a parasitic infection, is from undercooked and raw meat.

"The USDA (United States Department of Agriculture) is covering up the fact that the true cause of toxoplasmosis is not cats, but improperly cooked meat—from factory farming. Diseases like toxoplasmosis have become endemic in intensively raised animals.

25 percent of all pork and 10 percent of all lamb is infected with this parasite. Yet, the USDA doesn't warn people about that, it simply supports the system of intensive farming that causes health hazards," said the PETA spokesperson at a news conference, surrounded by a nurse, a mother with her newborn, and a pregnant woman in response to the USDA's accusations, detailed in Ingrid Newkirk's book, *Free The Animals.*

So how did this national fear campaign about cats and pregnant women sweep the nation?

The USDA was caught infecting kittens with toxoplasmosis.

"The more I see of men the more I like dogs."

Madame De Stael
French Writer
129

A student at the USDA's Beltsville Agricultural Research Center was horrified at the animal abuse and blew the whistle to ALF(Animal Liberation Front)documented in *Free The Animals,* along with their history and many other rescues.

ALF then sent an undercover agent into Beltsville to check out the story, and found: "...An Asian experimenter over there called Dr. J.P. Dubey. He does experiments on toxoplasmosis...He infects mice and then kills them and feeds their ground-up brains to cats.

The cats get sick and Dubey writes down their symptoms— diarrhea, dehydration, lung and intestinal tract infections. He's been doing that for fifteen years!"

In just one experiment... "He heavily infected eighty kittens by stomach tube..fifty-eight were one to five days of age."

In another experiment... "He's fed infected brain cysts to one-day old and one-week puppies and then killed them and examined their tissue.

Dubey reports getting his pregnant cats *from homes in Kansas City?*"

The ALF spy also witnessed mother pigs contained in *iron maidens*, which are tiny jails so small the pigs cannot even turn-around.

"There was a pig there who had been given the human growth gene in some kind of experiment (transgenics). He was hopelessly crippled, couldn't even stand."

ALF took action. Most animal research facilities are very respectable from the outside. Beltsville was no exception: the main facility was flanked by several outbuildings and lush grounds of green grass dotted with grazing cows and sheep. Most of the dirty work is conducted in the bowels of these buildings. Even the nearby creeks were polluted from Beltsville's agricultural chemicals.

ALF is headed by an ex-policeperson trained in England by the UK Animal Liberation Front, who became an animal welfare person after being involved in a Police Raid and witnessing terribly abused monkeys at the Institute for Behavioral Research.

The ALF breakout squad was briefed : "Toxoplasma...is a protozoan parasite, a single-celled organism sometimes contracted by eating raw or lightly cooked pork and other meats. Infections also occur in *cats* who *eat mice, rabbits*, and *birds*. But when contracted normally(as opposed to having mass quantities of the concentrated organism shot into their systems) the cats remain unaffected, shedding their larvae in their stools."

Employing night-vision glasses and approximately twelve trained liberators, ALF rescued 36 cats and several African miniature pigs from Beltsville Agricultural Research Center...all of which received veterinarian treatment before being relocated to loving homes.

"Mankind continues to become gradually less cruel because a few people in every generation keep saying, 'This isn't right. It hurts me to see it.'"

Joan Gilbert
American Author

But the USDA hit back fast and hard, the ramifications of which are still being felt today. ALF had penetrated their heavily guarded Beltsville Laboratories. They were furious. They were ready. They too had been trained in a series of seminars.
ALF had pulled-off many successful animal rescues and had made headway re-educating the public to counter the vivisectors' propaganda.

131

"If we are trespassing, so were the American Soldiers who broke down the gates of Hitler's death camps; If we are thieves, so were the members of the Underground Railroad who freed the slaves of the South; And if we are vandals, so were those who destroyed forever the gas chambers of Bucenwald and Auschwitz."

The Animal Rights Activist

PETA intercepted the fliers of several vivisector seminars, such as: *How To Handle A Break-in At Your Lab*. These seminars taught the vivisectors: *How To Take The Offensive*, and *Instituting Damage-Control* by spin-doctoring the media with the finesse of politicians. They recommended hiring pro-spin-doctors to protect their livelihoods and the millions of dollars at stake.

The vivisectors were instructed: (1) As soon as your animal laboratory is broken into contact the media ASAP, before the Animal Liberation Front (ALF) starts showing their photos of the abused animals they had rescued. Beat them to the punch. Every good propagandist knows: *first impressions are everything*.

(2) Use FEAR as the weapon: alarm the public; paint the Animal Welfare People as fanatics; pound home that the rescued animals carry transmittable diseases that the lab was working on curing so you and your family would be safe and healthy; we the vivisectors, are the good guys...we are your neighbors. We are the establishment.

"The belief in a supernatural source of evil is not necessary, men alone are quite capable of every wickedness."

Joseph Conrad
Polish Author

In direct response to ALF rescuing the cats at Beltsville that had been infected with toxoplasmosis by the USDA vivisectors (pigs were never addressed), the USDA issued a National Alert to scare pregnant women that their unborn babies' lives were endangered by cats carrying toxoplasmosis.

According to PETA's documentation, the toxoplasmosis alarm campaign and others that followed and continue to this day are carefully orchestrated PR campaigns taught in seminars, to destroy the growing Animal Welfare Movement.

PETA's response to the scare tactics was: "Whoever at the USDA has said toxoplasmosis is not treatable should be fired. Toxoplasmosis is not only easy to treat, it is easy to prevent." (*Especially if the USDA wasn't injecting animals with it.*)

PETA continued: "The USDA claims that its cat research is vital and aimed at treating humans and animals. In the fifteen years Dr. Dubey has conducted these experiments he has never once attempted to investigate or conduct any treatment of any human or animal.

His most important finding is that humans and cats should not eat *uncooked horsemeat*!

His second most important finding is that the greater the amount of *infected tissue you force into animals*, the greater their infection!"

Your tax dollars at work. Fifteen years of **intentionally** torturing **unconsenting** animals **unnecessarily** with zero results.

"It is easier to denature plutonium than to denature the evil spirit of man."

Albert Einstein

PETA ended their response to the USDA's National Toxoplasmosis Alert with: "Cats with toxoplasmosis can easily be treated, and no pregnant woman will be asked to handle these cats' feces with bare hands or to eat the animals. Therefore, no danger exists."

But PETA was not able to obtain the high profile media coverage of the USDA. The damage had been done, and persists to this day.

Many cats continue to be tossed out of formerly loving homes when the woman becomes pregnant, because of the misinformation from the USDA's PR campaign from the Beltsville rescue.

FACTS ON TOXOPLASMOSIS:

According to several reference books: Toxoplasmosis is a common parasitic infection in humans, warm-blooded animals and birds, transmitted by contact with the microorganism *toxplasma gondii.*

The symptoms usually resemble a cold.

Twenty-five percent of adults carry toxoplasmosis antibodies, meaning they were infected with toxoplasmosis at some point in their lives.

A single infection generally assures immunity.

The toxoplasmosis parasite is commonly found in cattle, poultry, and many domestic animals usually without harmful effects.

It continues to live in raw meat until the meat is cooked, dried, or frozen for extended periods of time.

The two main causes of toxoplasmosis infection are eating raw or undercooked meat, and direct contact with infected cat *feces* that is at least a day old.

Approximately 1 in 4,000 babies in the U.S. are born with birth defects from prenatal toxoplasmosis infection.

HOW TO PREVENT TOXOPLASMOSIS:

Pregnant women are most at risk. They should never eat undercooked or raw meat. Meat should be cooked thoroughly.

Only cats infected with toxoplasmosis they might have contracted from eating mice, rabbits, and birds are at risk.

Change litter boxes daily.
The oocytes in cat feces that causes toxoplasmosis do not become infected for two to four days.

If pregnant women change cat litter boxes, they should wear gloves. Small children should not play in uncovered sandboxes.

All feces from any animal or human is laden with bacteria. Proper hygiene, including vigorous hand-washing and not touching the face, prevents the spread of many infections.

"You're more likely to get sick from people than cats or any animals."

Dr. Donald Tede

Photo Obtained in 1999

Cat Intentionally Infected By Researchers

TRAPS, PETS & POTPOURRI

The Los Angeles Times reported, that according to a study conducted by The Journal of the American Medical Association, "Properly prescribed medications may kill more than 100,000 people a year...That would make adverse drug reactions between the sixth and fourth leading cause of death in the United States."

These are all drugs that have passed animal testing...which means many animals have suffered and died being fed overdoses that did not benefit humans.

"Routine medical monitoring, the standard of care for both human and non-human animals, is clearly not done, or is performed so carelessly that it would constitute medical malpractice in human patients...All in all, these studies demonstrate gross neglect and abuse of the laboratory subjects, results which are invalid, not only because of their poor applicability to human drug abuse, but due to uncontrolled variables of critical illness and inadequate medical monitoring of the animals."

Dr. Robin Ballina, MD

TRAPS

Cruel is too kind a word for leghold traps that lure hungry animals with food, then when the animal steps on them, steal clamps suddenly snap shut, grasping the animal's legs with jaw-like steel teeth. They are banned in 80 countries, but not in the U.S. and Canada.

137

In excruciating pain the animal will often chew off its limb(s) to free itself, only to die in the wild bleeding to death in sheer agony...this, so the trapper can sell the hide, or so we can wear the fur of the animals who don't chew themselves free...

"Man must practice kindness towards animals, for he who is cruel to animals becomes hard also in dealings with men. We can judge the heart of a man by his treatment of animals."

Immanuel Kant
German Philosopher

Snare traps or neck traps, have choked thousands of animals to death. Leghold and snare traps are outlawed in some states. Since 1990, animal welfare groups in the United States have successfully changed hunting and trapping laws in several states, by going directly to the voters through the initiative process with the aid of gruesome photos of actual trapped animals.

"All cruelty springs from weakness."

Seneca (4BC-65AD)

On January 1, 1996, the entire 15 countries comprising the European Union, banned the use of leghold traps and also the importation of fur from countries that use leghold traps.

U.S. and Canadian trappers export close to 70% of their fur to Europe. They are trying to circumvent the European ban on leghold traps by setting up vague humane standards that will still allow them to use agonizing leghold traps and continue to drown animals.

Trappers are currently pressuring the U.S. Trade Representative to help them bypass the European ban on leghold traps as a barrier to Free Trade, forbidden by the General Agreement on Tariffs and Trade(GATT).

Should this issue still be relevant, you can let your voice be heard in support of the European ban with a brief note: "Thank you for supporting the EU ban on leghold traps." U.S. Trade Representative, 6001 7th St., NW, Washington, D.C. 20506

"Custom will reconcile people to any atrocity; and fashion will drive them to acquire any custom."

George Bernard Shaw

In just California in 1997 alone, over 15,000 animals including pets(inadvertently), bobcats, foxes, and beavers were crushed in agonizing traps for their fur. In 1998, California voters approved a proposition to ban cruel and indiscriminate traps.

Under relentless pressure from animal welfare groups, the U.S. Department of Agriculture is attempting to design traps that will grasp animals while causing minimum pain...

LEATHER

Leather is typically a byproduct of the slaughterhouse. We have been using leather for over a half-million years. The process of turning animal hides into leather encompasses soaking, tanning, dyeing, drying, and polishing or finishing. Almost all leather produced in America is chrome-tanned. Chromium is classified as hazardous by the U.S. Environmental Agency(EPA).

Leather production also involves other pollutants such as: lead, formaldehyde, zinc, and cyanide based products.

There are many alternatives to leather, like canvas and Goretex, but some Goretex products are now mix-matching Goretex with leather, defeating the whole concept...

There are also now companies manufacturing faux leather that looks and feels just like real leather.

The downside is, some leather alternatives also pollute the environment, but at least the alternatives don't support animal suffering.

"An individual animal doesn't care if its species is facing extinction—it cares if it is feeling pain."

Ronnie Lee

Our industries are so interweaved, sometimes it's next to impossible to avoid all the animal byproducts that filter down from animal suffering...until the giants, vivisection and factory farming, go the way of public executions. When they fall, so will the byproducts.

Animal byproducts are so mixed into our everyday lives from honey, to silk clothing, to countless foods, to pet foods, even to the gelatin used to make photographic film--although there is now a gelatin film substitute but the price is prohibitive. But for computer users, there are digital film-less cameras.

Even the alcohol industry is tainted with animal byproducts. After wine's fermented, it is refined with ingredients such as: edible gelatins (animal bones), isinglass(fish bladders), casein and potassium caseinate(milk proteins) or animal albumin(egg albumin and dried blood powder).

Many beers are also refined with isinglass. Some bottled beers are not. Lagers and most hard liquors are usually animal free. Although some vodkas, do filter through bone charcoal. We all have to find our line of demarcation without becoming too eccentric or fanatic.

"Man is the only creature on Earth that tries to prove that it is different from, and preferably superior to, other species."

Paul Chance
Psychologist

Money is always the driving force. All business is based on profit. No profit, no business. Only the consumer switching off meat will eliminate factory farming. Meat sales are dropping, that's why the meat industry's PR mills are dragging out the same bogeymen they used for decades: The lie that humans need meat. *But now most educated people know humans don't need meat.*

Vegetarianism is a progressive process, so most people employed in these industries will be retired by attrition; unlike many of us who have experienced suddenly being downsized or fired because of corporate mergers, age discrimination, or any other excuse to cut cost and increase stock revenues.

Vivisection is also a specious, billion dollar business woven into our infrastructure, that won't go down without a vicious fight to maintain the sinister status quo experimenting on animals. As long as the money keeps flowing in...Vivisectors will *intentionally* and *unnecessarily* inflict pain on *unconsenting* non-human-animals.

"Beware of false prophets(vivisectors), who come to you in sheep's clothing, but inwardly they are ravenous wolves."
Jesus Christ

Vivisectors never learn, because they never have to pay the price they have made millions of animals pay. Just the opposite: they get rewarded with accolades and comfortable lifestyles.

Their painful and killing experiments are always at the expense of other living animals, under the guise of *causing pain for the greater good.*

Vivisectors should persuade the government to allow them to conduct their experiments on themselves or colleagues who volunteer. Fat chance. They would never undergo the experiments they submit others too...But people who are dying, would gladly volunteer to try some potentially hopeful treatment. 141

The same goes for doctors who injected plutonium and uranium for decades into unsuspecting people under government directives; doctors and officials who would never inject themselves to test anything.

The same as government leaders who declare wars...let them go first, and there would be no wars. Hawks with *You Go Mentality*.

Like vivisectors, others always pay the price for their pompous ideas. If their schemes are so wonderful they should be the guinea pigs.

"That which seems to be at the height of absurdity in one generation often becomes the height of wisdom in another."

Adlai Stevenson

Because of millions of your tax dollars at stake for their previously mentioned, red-hot Frankenstein science, Xenotransplants: transplanting animal cells, organs, tissues, marrow, etc. Vivisectors have set the stage for Armageddon with the animal welfare groups...

Lobbyists and spokespeople for the vivisectors are conducting fever-pitched PR campaigns that these animal transplants will save (prolong) your life; but in my opinion they are from the darkside and will eventually fail and cause thousands or millions of more animals to suffer needlessly; but the vivisectors are plunging $-ahead-$ despite the dangers of transmitting more diseases like AIDS from monkeys, certain viruses from pigs, and even the Ebola Virus is thought to have jumped from primates to humans.

"The decent moderation of today will be the least of human things tomorrow. At the time of Spanish Inquisition, the opinion of good sense and of the good medium was certainly that people ought not to burn too large a number of heretics."

Maurice Maeterlinck
Belgium Playwright & Poet

PETA has obtained inside information that well-connected vivisectors are so worried their occupations will go the way of the slave traders and child labor employers, that they have mounted a relentless media offensive. Their medical PR is reported with the news as news, and some people don't realize the hungry media is fed these Medical Press Releases by the vivisectors to continue obtaining your tax dollars.

"Crank—a man with a new idea until it succeeds."

Mark Twain

One interagency memorandum PETA intercepted from the National Institute of Mental Health (NIMH)stated: "The stakes are enormous. The animal rights movement threatens the very core...The bunker strategy is no longer tenable."

The above memorandum goes on to solicit help from all vivisectors whose livelihoods are threatened to join together, in particularly the all powerful American Medical Association(AMA), and other researchers involved in healthcare, to obliterate the animal welfare movement.

Go "proactive..." establish a "counter-educational effort..." with the AMA and the Department of Education to garner "public and congressional support... draw up a list of such illnesses and the (animal) research upon which treatment is dependent. Whenever feasible, the research institutions should leave the out front activities to the other groups."

The memorandum even offers "financial incentives" to destroy the credibility of the animal welfare groups.

This particular memorandum, documented in the book *Free The Animals,* was written by Dr. Frederick Goodwin when he headed NIMH and was forwarded to the Foundation for Biomedical Research, established by the Charles River Breeding Company, the

143

world's largest animal breeder for experimentation—and financed by the mammoth pharmaceutical and cosmetic corporations still experimenting on animals.

"As long as human beings go on shedding the blood of animals, there will never be any peace.

Isaac Bashevis Singer

PETS

Pets are great for companionship, and dependent on human kindness. Pets should be treated with love and kept in appropriate environments.

"One of the most dangerous things that can happen to a child is to kill or torture an animal and get away with it."

Margaret Mead

The *number one dog trainer in America* for two years running, does not believe in ever hitting his dogs or training like a Drill Sergeant. He teaches only from the kindness of the positive-reinforcement-reward-system. He never reprimands or is mean to his dogs. He states his only secret is: *love and positive reinforcement*. He says he always knew in his heart that mean-training was wrong, so he set out to prove his intuition right. A dog's main aim is to please its owner.

"Murderers often start out by killing and torturing animals as kids."

Robert K. Resler
Serial Killer Profiler for the FBI

In 88% of New Jersey families being treated for child abuse, animals in the home had been abused, according to a recent article. Children in violent homes often participate in pecking-order battering and maim or kill an animal who is powerless.
144

Monty Roberts, the man the novel and the movie The *Horse Whisper* was based on, dedicated his life to re-educating horse owners to employ love and gently train their horses. He was livid at untrue horse-breaking scene in the movie and fought to no avail to have it altered. "The producers told me that they were gonna lay this horse down with love, care and concern. And I said: 'When you go home tonight will you tie your wife down with love, care and concern? Walk around her to get up, to be *subservient to you*? I trained with love.'"

Our pets lives are so short, most of them learn to know what is expected almost through osmosis. Absolutely no cruelty is justified.

A big dog left in a tiny apartment all day and expected not to go the bathroom, is not kind. Try it sometime...

Some people even lock their pets in the bathroom all day while they go to work. How would they like being locked in a tiny room all day? Or leaving a dog chained.

Where there's a will, there's always a kinder way...

In the United Kingdom it's against the law for veterinarians to de-claw cats. It's like pulling out our fingernails. It's horrendous and leaves the cat defenseless.

"Do unto others as you want done unto you."
                                    Golden Rule of Most Religions

Puppy-mills are factory farmed puppies. At a few weeks old these puppies are crammed into trailer trucks to pet stores across the country. Some do not survive the transport. And many of those who do survive, have health and emotional problems, because of the puppy-mills' heartless handling and squalid conditions. Puppy-millers should be dealt stiff criminal penalties.

Some breeders also over-breed, which typically involves interbreeding and makes the pet a distorted caricature of hirself(unisex gender), and susceptible to a hosts of physical and psychological conditions and diseases. Over-breeding should be forbidden for the same reasons human interbreeding is an abomination.

"The assumption that animals acted exclusively by instinct, while man had a monopoly on reason, is, we think, maintained by few people nowadays who have any knowledge at all about animals. We can only wonder that so absurd a theory could have been held for so long a time as it was, when on all sides the evidence of animals' power of reasoning is crushing."

Ernest Bell

Dog fighting matches are back with a vengeance. Pitbulls are the most common dog breed used in this gambling-driven-horror-show. The dogs are trained in bloodthirsty conditions to fight to the death, incurring fifty or more fatal bite-wounds. Small dogs are frequently stolen and sacrificed as training- bait, to taunt the pitbulls and other fighting dogs into becoming more vicious.

Children and pets are both at our mercy. The penalty for conducting dog fights should be mandatory jail time with no parole.

"Out of 135 violent criminals, 118 admitted that when they were children they burned, hanged and stabbed domestic animals."

Ogonyok (Russian Magazine)

By its nature a bird is meant to fly, not to live as a prisoner in a tiny cage for our amusement.

"A bird in the hand is a certainty, but a bird in the bush may sing."

Bret Harte
American Author

146

In most cases it's selfish not to leave wild animals in the wild and protect their environments. But once we have taken them out of their environment into ours, like good parents we are then responsible to treat them kindly.

"Only that thing is free which exists by the necessities of its own nature, and is determined in its actions by itself alone."
Spinoza
Dutch Theologian & Philosopher

Anthropomorphism is a termed often hurled at animal lovers by people exploiting animals for money or their amusement.

It's meant to be an insult, but it's a compliment: compassion and love are our best qualities.

Anthropomorphism, relatively speaking, is attributing human (as if we're so wonderful) qualities to animals. I think it's an insult to the animals. Humans play, feel, procreate, suffer and die... so do animals.

"There is no fundamental difference between man and the higher mammals in their mental faculties...The difference in mind between man and the higher animals...certainly is one of degree and not of kind."
Charles Darwin

FOOD FOR THOUGHT
In Korea, Thailand, and Vietnam, etc. dog meat is considered a delicacy and sought after for its health benefits and as an aphrodisiac. It cost the same as beef. The dog hides are prized and sold.

Their spokespeople are constantly carping that Western meat eaters employ a double-standard and are hypocrites for judging them. They claim if you didn't know you were eating dog, you'd think it was beef. Cannibals might make the same claims...In some countries they eat U. S. horsemeat as a gourmet meat since 1986, which is the money-driving force to slaughter wild horses, which is done by driving a spike into the horse's head, hanging hir(unsex gender) upside down, then dismembering hir while still alive.

"Man is the only creature endowed with the power of laughter; is he not also the only one that deserves to be laughed at?"

Sir Richard Grenville
English Naval Officer

Pets On Stage is a popular stage show hosting a hodge-podge of big and little dogs and cats performing amazing acrobatic feats. Joe Slater is the CEO. He finds all his actors and actresses at the pound. "I try to rescue the oldest and hardest to handle dogs and cats that I don't think anybody will adopt. Then I give them lots of love and attention and find out what acrobatic stunts they might enjoy performing. You can see watching them grandstand, how thrilled and how much fun they are having. That's how I train. *By fun and positive reinforcement.*"

TEN COMMANDMENTS FOR A RESPONSIBLE PET OWNER

(SPCA of Texas)

1. My life is likely to last 10 to 15 years. Any separation from you will be very painful.

2. Give me time to understand what you want of me.

3. Place your trust in me—it is crucial for my well-being.

4. Don't be angry with me for long, and don't lock me up as punishment. You have your work, your friends, your entertainment. I HAVE ONLY YOU!

5. Talk to me. Even if I don't understand your words, I understand your voice when it's speaking to me.

6. Be aware that however you treat me, I'LL NEVER FORGET IT!

7. Before you hit me, remember that I have teeth that could easily crush your bones in your hand, but I choose not to bite you.

8. Before you scold me for being lazy or uncooperative, ask yourself if something might be bothering me. Perhaps I'm not getting the right food, I've been out in the sun too long, or my heart may be getting old and weak.

9. Take care of me when I get old. You, too, will grow old.

10. Go with me on difficult journeys. Never say, "I can't bear to watch it," or "Let it happen in my absence." Everything is easier for me if YOU are there. RE-MEMBER, I LOVE YOU!

HELL HOLES & SAVIORS

"I am not basically a conservationist. I am not concerned about the wiping out of a species—this is man's folly—I have one concern, the suffering which we deliberately inflict upon animals while they live."

Clive Hollands

BOYS TOWN GONE BAD

An undercover investigation by PETA at the world famous Boys Town in Nebraska, would have poor Father Flanagan turning over in his grave.

Boys Town's National Research Hospital landed $3 million of your tax dollars to torture and mutilate cats.

"Staff experimenter Glenn R. Farley starved 42 cats until they lost 20% of their body weight. The reason? To make them cry! Farley claimed to be developing a model for vocal tract control.

After six months of hunger(called training) Farley implanted a T-shaped tube in each cat's throat and hooked wires to their muscles so that he could record the animals' cries.

He then screwed a metal device into the cats' skull and cemented it in place so that he could immobilize the animals by attaching their heads to a stationary frame."

PETA continues: "One of our investigators found that Boys Town husband-and-wife vivisecting team Edward J. Walsh and JoAnn McGee sliced open kittens' heads and cut the nerves in their brains. Why? To learn more about how the ear works.

Most of the kittens die because they are so young (some are mutilated the day they're born) that they can't survive the trauma."

PETA concludes: "Experts have condemned the experiments as both painful and useless. Dr. Robert S. Hoffman, a neurologist wrote, 'I am offended...when I see public money being diverted from important public works to projects like this, which seem designed purely to satisfy the curiosity of (experimenters) and advance their academic careers.'"

"It's a matter of taking the side of weak against the strong, something the best people have always done."

Harriet Beecher Stowe

PETA's undercover investigation, documented Boys Town vivisectors failed to provide veterinary care for the animals they made sick, and didn't use any postsurgical painkillers, which is even in violation of federal law.

Boys Town vivisectors attempted to vindicate themselves, claiming they starved cats, implanted tubes and wires in their throats, cemented metal devices into their skulls, sliced open kittens' heads to cut the nerves in their brains...to cure deafness.

The World Federation of the Deaf has condemned Boys Town experiments as wasteful and cruel.

PAWS

PAWS((Performing Animal Welfare Society) claims to be "the only society dedicated to the rescue of performing and exotic animals from cruel confinement and performances of pain," founded by former Hollywood trainer and author Pat Derby, and her partner Ed Stewart.

152

Pat Derby was a sought after exotic animal trainer for top TV shows like Flipper, Daktari, Gunsmoke, Lassie, Disney movies, and commercials like the Lincoln-Mercury cougars.

Unlike other trainers, who were using clubs, prods or hooks to make animals perform, Pat trained with kindness, resourcefulness and patience, but at that time the business of Hollywood would have none of it.

"I loved working with animals. That's what I wanted to do. But when animals are a business, animals suffer. You do what you have to do to get the shot."

Pat Derby

Pat and her partner Ed established PAWS in Galt, near Sacramento, California, to be close to the State Legislature, so she could petition for new animal protection laws against electric shocking, food deprivation, and other physical and psychological punishments used in training, and to restrict the ownership and breeding of wild animals.

PAWS is a 20-acre sanctuary where discarded animals call home and live unchained: eight lions, four tigers, seven monkeys, six bears (Lennie a Disney bear), two wolves, a wallaby, a leopard, a bobcat, a baboon (many TV credits), a tamarin and an ostrich as of this writing.

A few discarded animals still come from Hollywood, but most of the unwanted animals now come from circuses, zoos, and private parties who have abused them. Like Denny, Max and Fifer, three teenage lion clubs and former pets, whose owners ripped their claws out with pliers, tearing out some of the paw with it, so Denny has stubs instead of front feet.

"Man is condemned to be free; because once thrown into the world, he is responsible for everything he does."

Jean-Paul Sartre
French Philosopher & Author

GOVERNMENT CONTINUES TO FUND CRUELTY

The National Institute of Health(NIH) continues to dole out your tax dollars to known cruel researchers like Dr. Ronald Woods, awarded a grant of more than $400,000 for disease research, after being charged by the U.S. Department of Agriculture with hundreds of cruel violations while at New York University, such as: strapping monkeys into restraining chairs, placing the monkeys into old refrigerators and forcing them to inhale the fumes of crack cocaine, etc. A surprise investigation found three monkeys dead from abuse, lack of veterinary care, and no water.

"Anyone who has accustomed himself to regard the life of any living creature as worthless is in danger of arriving also at the idea of worthless human lives."

Dr. Albert Schweitzer

FARM SANCTUARY

Farm Sanctuary is a 175-acre oasis in upstate New York for abused or badly injured farm animals. It was established by Lorri and Gene Bauston, after stumbling onto a living ewe cast onto a pile of animals who had died from being trucked in humid-heat over 100 degrees.

Lorri and Gene were researching the food industry, and by coincidence came upon Hilda on a heap of dead animals in a Pennsylvanian stockyard. "Her head was lying limply over the edge of a cement slab on which she had been thrown, just inches from a rotting carcass. Flies and maggots were crawling all over her body."

The Bauston's went on to save Hilda and found the trucker who dumped her the day before, but were shocked it was standard procedure to crowd hundreds of animals onto trucks, then just before they reach their destination, dump the lame and dead animals that succumb during transit.

They were even more shocked the county animal anti-cruelty representative nor the District Attorney would prosecute: "normal animal agricultural practices" are exempt from animal cruelty laws.

Hence Farm Sanctuary, the first and largest farm animal sanctuary came into being. Today the Baustons have over 300 discarded farm animals: cattle, sheep, goats, chickens, turkeys, pigs, rabbits, ducks, and geese.

They now also have a Farm Sanctuary West in Orland (near Sacramento), California.

"...The deer, the horse, the great eagle, these are our brothers. The rocky crests, the juices in the meadows, the body heat of the pony and man—all belong to the same family...The White Man must treat the beasts of this land as his brothers."

Chief Seattle

HENRY VILAS ZOO TORMENTING PRIMATES

The Henry Vilas Zoo in Madison, Wisconsin had an agreement with the University of Wisconsin Primate Research Center, that their rhesus monkeys would be used in non-invasive research.

However, *dozens* of the monkeys were subjected to experiments that ended with their deaths. Animal welfare groups partitioned the NIH, which was funding the experiments with your tax dollars. NIH stated there was no justification and eliminated funding. The remaining 142 rhesus monkeys were reportedly sent to a sanctuary, rather than being sold to Tulane University for more experiments, like the University of Wisconsin requested.

"We were put here to build, not to destroy."

Red Skelton

ASSOCIATION OF VETERINARIANS FOR ANIMAL RIGHTS(AVAR)

Mission Statement: "AVAR is the only veterinarian medical association actively promoting rights for non-human animals," es-

155

tablished by Neil C. Wolff, D.V.M. and Nedim C. Buyukmihci, V.M.D., because "the veterinary profession, under the banner of adequate veterinary care often supported practices which were completely contradictory to the well-being of the animals."

AVAR is against vivisection on moral grounds: it believes non-human animals and human animals have a right to their own independent interests and lives.

AVAR also opposes non-human animals for food and fiber, and advocates a vegetarian lifestyle. So animals can "enjoy their brief lives."

The American Veterinary Association, the mother of veterinarian organizations believes in using animals as tools for humans, so does not support AVAR: "We cannot endorse the philosophical views and personal values of animal rights advocates when they are incompatible with the responsible use of animals for human purposes."

The American Veterinary Association also supports all animal testing, and doesn't endorse the existing non-animal alternatives for most research, testing, and educational uses.

AVAR is opposed to using animals as tools for all medical education and offers schools and individuals free: "Electronic databases of audiovisual and textual materials, computer programs, simulators and models, which can be used as alternatives to the harmful or destructive use of non-human animals in all levels of education."

"We must do all in our power to educate the public, for I believe that in the end, only a change of heart is really effective."

Ruth Harrison

WAR ON WESTERN HORSES
Wild horses were a symbol of the freedom the Wild West offered humans. A second chance at life to make it right.

At the dawn of this century there were 2 million horses roaming the Western United States. There are now estimated to be only 46,000 left. Horses and burros were routinely slaughtered for money until Congress finally passed the Wild Free Roaming Horse and Burro Act, unfortunately for the horses, Congress place their fate with the Bureau of Land Management(BLM).

Using your tax dollars, the BLM was bullied by cattle ranchers and others with financial interests, to remove the remaining horses from their habitats and let their cattle graze the subsidized land into irreversible dust bowls.

According to PETA: "Livestock-raising accounts for 85 percent of topsoil loss in the United States." Horses are nomadic and usually never overgraze.

The BLM decided to enact a disastrous adoption policy for these wild horses. Using helicopters and cowboys they rounded-up over 141,762 horses for auction.

PETA states: "The weakest, sickest, and oldest were rounded-up first, since the contractors are paid per horse and these are the easiest to catch. These wild horses suffered the physical and psychological trauma of being run for several miles, confined, auctioned, transported, and forever separated from members of their families and herds."

So far over 60,000 wild horses have been adopted, and more than 10,000 horses at time were held in holding pens at a cost of almost $18 million a year of your tax dollars.

At this point, $100 million of your tax dollars has funded this failed and cruel adoption program.

The BLM was caught adopting out over 20,000 horses for free, and adopting out more than four horses at a time (violating the rule of four horses to a family for $125. a horse), to people who in turn sold the horses for $250. each to slaughterhouses.

"A single rancher obtained 400 free horses, 110 of whom were later starved to death," said PETA.

In response to petitions from animal welfare groups, a federal judge in Reno ruled the mass adoptions were completely contrary to the original idea of wild horse protection and ordered the BLM to stop the mass adoption policy.

The BLM attempted to go against the judges orders and continue their mass adoption, but several animal protection groups and the federal government stopped them.

The BLM's best idea has probably been the contraception of the remaining wild horse herds, but it's only been a half-hearted effort.

The BLM's energy and interest appears to be with the cattle ranchers. In a report to the Academy of Sciences, the BLM attempted to blame the wild horses for the topsoil erosion caused by the cattle, but failed to demonstrate that the wild horses had caused any significant damage.

PETA contends that, "The BLM is driven to pursue their interference with the wild horses, and is currently contracting taxpayer-funded, wild horse sanctuaries for unadoptable horses without any workable plan for self-sufficiency."

An Associated Press(AP) story stated, "Federal agents, already catching heat for allowing the slaughter of thousands of wild horses, gave false information to Congress this year while trying to prove aggressive enforcement of a law meant to protect the animals... AP found only three convictions.

'Without enforcement there's no teeth. It's a joke,' said Dale Tunnel, a retired BLM law enforcement official.

AP has reported many people who adopt wild horses or burros under the $16 million-a-year program (your tax dollars) could not account for their animals, that thousands ended up in slaughterhouses..."

"In the end we must, I think, somehow conclude that the animals have as much right to this planet as we have."

Prince Philip
Duke of Edinburgh

In 1998, Californians approved a proposition to criminalize the slaughter of horses for sale as horsemeat for human consumption. In the last decade, 2.5 million horses nationwide have been slaughtered(four inch spike into the horse's head, then hung upside down, bled and dismembered while still alive) for human consumption in foreign countries. But the Californian ballot measure ironically didn't protect horsemeat from its largest market--pet food.

MONKEY SANCTUARY

Monkey Sanctuary is the first place where monkeys rescued from zoos or as pets could live a natural life in an outside simulated habitat, was established in 1964 by Leonard Williams in the United Kingdom.

The Monkey Sanctuary today is owned and operated by the keepers. All profits are used for the benefit of this beautiful species of woolly monkeys.

"The establishment of the common origin of all species logically involves a readjustment of altruistic morals, by enlarging the application of what has been called the Golden Rule from the area of mere mankind to that of the whole animal kingdom."

Thomas Hardy
English Author

NAVY CONTINUES BAD WAYS

The U.S. Navy continues exploiting animals. One of the Navy's sonar research programs, blasted high volume sounds from the Whale Marine Sanctuary at humpback whales during their mating season off the Hawaiian Islands. The blasts were so deafening, some marine biologists said it could have seriously harmed or killed some whales.

"The majority is always wrong...That's why we have the Bill of Rights, to protect the minority."

S. Francis

CHIMPANZEE RETIREMENT SYSTEM

Your tax dollars are currently supporting animal research on about 1700 chimpanzees across the U.S. Once the chimps complete a battery of vaccine testings or other grant-funded experiments, the ones who survive are no longer useful to researchers. No $-grant-$ money, suddenly the vital experiments are no longer necessary.

Hundreds of these aging chimps, who have lifespans similar to humans if they survive the experiments, sit caged for decades in windowless, concrete laboratories, pulling out their fur, waiting to die.

The **National Antivivisection Society(NAVS)** is spearheading a coalition of animal advocacy groups to establish a number of sanctuaries, such as **Primarily Primates** in San Antonio, Texas, that petitioned for the famous Buckshire 12: a dozen chimps that had been raised in laboratory cages and served as biomedical research subjects, performed in roadside circuses, and lived as pets till they grew up and became *chimps*...all became property of the Buckshire Corporation, a large animal brokerage company that

160

normally would have re-adopted them out for more laboratory experiments, but after being petitioned, offered to give the chimps up to this wonderful sanctuary.

Many of the laboratory chimps had never experienced fresh air or the warmth of sunlight till they arrived free in Primarily Primates. Dr. Jane Goodall is working with NAVS to help design the national sanctuary system.

"Science is just catching up to the person in the street, who knows animals feel the same range of emotions as us."

Diane Sawyer
TV Show Turning Point

The **Fauna Foundation in Carignan**, Quebec, Canada, began when Gloria Grow had a conscience crisis on her 40th birthday. She was a former groomer and animal welfare activist, who with her veterinarian partner Richard Allan, decided to offer refuge to chimps who formally had been experimented on in U.S. laboratories (there is currently a moratorium in Canada), or were cast off from circuses or as pets. The Foundation also is home to a menagerie of 400 other discarded animals including ostriches and pot-pellied pigs.

Her first shipment of chimps came from New York University's Laboratory of Experimental Medicine and Surgery. Victoria says the abused chimps came with thick horror files. Many were in their teens or 20s. The chimps average lifespan is 60-plus.

Billy Jo and Sue Ellen were two chimps that arrived HIV-positive thanks to vivisectors injecting them with the virus. They were as inseparable as youngsters. Donna Rae also arrived injected with the HIV virus. She had been a family pet who played the guitar and rode a bicycle at parties. At the age of 12, holding her owner's hand, she was walked into the NYU laboratory, and left there with the research vivisectors...

161

Then there was Yoko, a small wiry chimp in perpetual motion--Her file stated she had undergone 137 experimental liver biopsies... And Regis, a playful 9 year old still has number 645 tattooed on his chest. His file states he was knocked down, which means large doses of experimental tranquilizers were forced into him until he collapsed over 279 times...

And Jeannie's file says she is *crazy* because she bites herself incessantly after snapping during an AIDS experiment.

"One act of pure love in saving life is greater than spending the whole of one's time in religious offerings to the gods."

Dhammanpada(Buddhist)

PAIN RELIEF VICTORY

Feeling the sales' $$$ heat from animal welfare groups against trapping, Sears has drastically reduced the amount of fur trimmed garments they sell.

CIRCUSES NO FUN FOR ANIMALS

The King Royal Circus and Ringling Brothers Circuses have both repeatedly been found guilty of animal cruelty. Such as the neglected elephant found dead in the trailer of The King Royal Circus, which had already been cited numerously for animal abuse. And thankfully a Ringling whistleblower contacted PETA, who alerted the USDA, that a known sick baby elephant was forced to perform. The baby elephant died shortly after the performance and Ringling tried to truck his body away but got caught.

PET THERAPY

My wife is an Activity Director for a convalescent home. She says pet visits is one of the favorite activities that residents look forward to. Even residents who are normally withdrawn begin to open up with big smiles and hidden love to pat and hug the puppies, kittens, dogs, cats, etc. that the volunteers might bring to cheer them up.

Darrian Lundy, a Pet Therapist for the Delta Society agrees. "It (pet visits) gets people talking who haven't talked all week."

Darrian brings chickens that won't end up on anybody's dinner table, for therapeutic sessions at convalescent homes. She begins their training at one week old by hand-feeding them and getting them use to walking on a leash, till they respond to just a harness, so she can pass the chickens around to the patients.

One resident who had been raised on a farm said, "It's unusual to find a chicken so calm," as she stroked Spock's feathers. Her feather-mate, Chickadee, was strutting around for the other patients amusement at the time.

Harley, Darrian's pig, also likes to visit the elderly but prefers escorting Darrian alone, rather than sharing the spotlight with any chickens.

"Animals have their tragic and their comic side, and resemble us in many ways. They, too, have their distinctions and individualities. Many people believe that there is a huge gap separating them from the animals, but it is only really a step in the Wheel of Life, for we are all children of the One. To understand a fellow creature, we must regard him as a brother."

Manfred Kyber

NASA'S FLIGHTS OF HELL

All the wrong stuff: PETA has received several conscience calls from NASA employees, enumerating several monkey deaths at NASA's Ames Research Center, from inept surgeries and poor post-surgical care. Employees also detailed monkeys ripping out electrode wires beneath their skin, causing hideous and chronic infections... And monkeys dying of dehydration from careless workers who didn't even check their clogged sipper tubes.

163

NASA routinely drills holes in animals' skulls and sinks electrodes in their brains, when the tests are completed the animals are decapitated in a guillotine called an animal dispatcher without any anesthesia.

One of NASA's many boondoggles to snag money was launching a $32 million joint U.S./French/Russian space flight called Bion 11 and 12, even though NASA already had the same weightless data on human beings who had spent more than 400 days in space. Bions are antiquated Russian capsules, that NASA employees say were not even correctly equipped to record the data.

Insiders informed PETA, that Bions' space experiments forced monkeys to sustain agonizing, invasive procedures. Fourteen electrode wires were sunk into seven muscles in the monkeys' arms and legs that burrowed under their skin and exited from a hole cut in their backs. More electrodes were inserted into the monkeys' brains—their exposed skulls were covered with metal caps and eight holes were drilled into their skulls to accommodate a plastic halo so they couldn't move their heads. Other wires from a surgically buried thermometer in each animals' abdomen, exited a second hole carved in the monkeys' backs. NASA employees stated that several of the tests monkeys' mutilated themselves trying to rip the wires out, despite the attempt of NASA vivisectors, who bound the animals in straightjackets.

Multik, was one of the tortured, electrode-implanted monkeys, whose tail had been amputated so he could be strapped into a restraining chair for the two week launch...he was released from his suffering, when he died in less than 24-hours after returning to earth.

The Bion launches occurred, despite PETA notifying neurologists who condemned the cruelty and even the House of Representatives who voted to cut all funding to the Bion project.

164

"It takes a lot more courage to go against the herd and be a pacifist, than to be a warrior who just goes along with the crowd."

S. Francis

PIGS SANCTUARY

Dale Riffle and Jim Brewer rescued a small piglet only to discover the local rescues didn't accept homeless pigs--hence they formed PIGS, a farm outside Washington D.C., which is home or a way station to a good home for thousands of abused, abandoned, and neglected pot-bellied pigs.

PIGS also educates people to the plight of pot-bellies, that were the hot rage for the exotic animal industry a few years back. The sanctuary also provides a home for other victim animals that find their way to PIGS.

"Our treatment of animals will someday be considered barbarous. There cannot be perfect civilization until man realizes that the rights of every living creature are as sacred as his own."

Dr. David Starr Jordan

WARDEN DENTIST

Many people don't like going to the dentists. Dr. Patrick Fleege of Seattle, offers justification.

For over two decades Dr. Patrick imprisoned PJ, a capuchin monkey in a small plexiglas box inside his dental office. At night, PJ was taken from the plexiglas box, put in a cage, and placed in a storage closet for the night. At the time of this writing, Wildlife Rescue and Rehabilitation(WRR) was attempting to pressure Dr. Fleege to release PJ to them.

"Cruelty to animals is one of the best examples of the continuity of psychological disturbances from childhood to adulthood."

Cornell University of Veterinary Medicine

165

JES Exotic

A 10-acre sanctuary in rural Wisconsin for lions, tigers, leopards, cougars, bears, horses, cows, foxes, and other misfits, established by Jill E. Shumak and her family after she mistakenly attempted to become a breeder of large cats.

"We were under the misconception that breeding large felids was an appropriate endeavor. Fortunately, we found out how wrong we were before we brought any into the world."

But many big cats that have no other place to go, end up at Jill's sanctuary.

"We have tried finding homes for and placing large cats with disastrous results," said Jill. "The animals we have placed in what we believed to be safe, humane homes were horribly abused.
We do not find homes for animals here. This is their home, their last stop and their last chance."

"If the single man plant himself indomitably on his instincts, and there abide, the huge world will come round to him."

Emerson

MICKEY MOUSES' HEARTLESS FATHER

Disneyland has made millions as the home of the most famous mouse in history. But according to PETA, Disneyland continues to use glue-traps, deemed by some the cruelest of mousetraps, despite many humane live-traps available. Rodents caught in a glue-trap bite into their limbs attempting to free themselves. Some get their faces stuck in the glue and slowly suffocate, the rest starve and thirst to death in terror.

Rodent populations are easily controlled by sanitary conditions and plugging holes of entry.

Humane traps allow the catcher to remove the problem and release the animals unharmed back in nature.

Two years of protests did not moved the multi-billion dollar corporation. Ironically, Walt Disney the founder, lived most of his life pursuing his dream burdened with debt, and was reported to be an animal lover.

"Love of animals is a universal impulse, a common ground on which all of us may meet. By loving and understanding animals, perhaps we humans shall come to understand each other."

Dr. Louis J. Camuti

DONKEY SANCTUARY

Donkey Sanctuary is a refuge for donkeys at risk in the United Kingdom and Ireland. It was established after Welfare Officers throughout the UK and Ireland were called to investigate severe donkey abuse.

The Donkey Sanctuary educates people in donkey care to help reduce cruelty through ignorance and offers abused or homeless donkeys a permanent home in their sanctuary if they can't find a suitable home.

Any potential foster parent must attend a donkey care course, and have their homes inspected regularly by Welfare Officers to check on the donkey's well-being. If the officers find the new home unfit, the donkey is returned to the sanctuary.

"All the arguments to prove man's superiority cannot shatter this hard fact: in suffering the animals are our equals."

Pete Singer

WHOLE BODY TRANSPLANTS

Touted on ABC News: *Whole Body Transplants* (being conducted on monkeys). These gruesome, useless experiments are

167

being conducted by Dr. Robert White of Case Western Reserve University in Cleveland, Ohio.

Dr. White has been conducting his research for many years, states PETA. He admits that these experiments are impossible to perform on humans, yet he continues to do them on monkeys, none of whom have survived more than a week of this crippling and beheading torture. Countless animals have suffered in his laboratory and millions of dollars have been wasted.

Following the ABC news story, San Francisco radio station KGO interviewed Dr. White, who bragged about the millions of dollars of influx grant money(your tax dollars) for spinal research because of celebrity Christopher Reeves' tragedy.

He spoke of whole body transplants he and the other vivisectors were now experimenting with, by severing the heads of healthy monkeys and attaching them onto the torso's of other formally healthy but now crippled and decapitated monkeys...the radio commentator boasted about his guest, an American doctor, being a devout Catholic and confidante of the Pope. Guess they forget Noah saved the animals...I'm sure St. Francis will be waiting to greet him.

"He who harms animals has not understood or renounced deeds of sin...Those whose minds are at peace and who are free from passions do not desire to live at the expense of others."

Acharagga Sutra(Jainism)

DUCK DEFENCE OF SOUTH AUSTRALIA

According to the Duck Defence, every year in Australia there are hundreds of thousands of ducks left maimed and wounded by duck hunters. The Duck Defence Coalition rescues and attempts to treat the wounds of as many ducks as possible. They also strive to educate the public "to lobby to stop this barbarism."

"Man cannot pretend to be higher in ethics, spirituality, advancement, or civilization than other creatures, and at the same time live by lower standards than the vulture or hyena."

H.J. Dinsah

168

THE GREYHOUND PROJECT

Finds homes "for the fastest friend you'll ever have," says Dan Schmidt, who runs the adoption project for these retired racing dogs out of the Washington D.C. area.

The Greyhound is thought to be oldest domestic dog, dating back 8,000 years to early cave drawings, and was esteemed by the ancient Egyptians and Celts.

"The soul is the same for all living creatures, although the body of each is different."

Hippocrates

WILD FELINE RESCUE

Rick Leither was a compassionate veterinarian for decades. These days he and his wife Carol, find homes for homeless felines in Cresecent City, CA. Even when the Humane Society temporarily closed, the Leithers took in their 40 cats, to add to their already full house of 200 felines, before finding homes for 95 of them.

Rick has been featured on Good Morning America and the Dan Rather News Show, accompanied by his buddy Scooter, a former abandoned kitten, with paralzyed back legs. Dr. Rick constructed a lightweight cart that enables Scooter to run and play with all the other cats. Scooter doesn't even know he's handicapped.

"He is very imprudent, a dog: he never makes it his business to inquire whether you are in the right or the wrong, never asks whether you are rich or poor, silly or wise, sinner or saint. You are his pal. That is enough for him."

Jerome K. Jerome

DALMATIANS ResQ

Randy Warner, a former Las Vegas computer programmer, is the first to admit how silly it is to live with 27 Dalmatians. But he's on a mission: 12,000 Dalmatians a year end up at the pound, many from owners Randy claims, who failed to beat their hyperactivity out of them.

"It's a situation humans created, and humans, ultimately must be held accountable for. When you adopt a dog, you're making a commitment for 15 years. If you're 21 or 22, you're not qualified for a dog. Don't adopt a dog until you've settled into your life. Two dogs provide each other company, and are literally half the trouble as one. They've been waiting all day and when you walk in they want to play and you're exhausted. That won't happen if there is another dog at home."

An estimated 27 million unwanted dogs are put to sleep each year in U.S. pounds.

"We need a moral philosophy in which the concept of love, so rarely mentioned now by philosophers, can once again be made central."

Iris Murdoch

Most of these and many more sanctuaries, and most animal welfare organizations and societies now have internet web-sites. You should be able to find them by typing their name into an internet search engine(an online directory), which will bring you to their web-site(s).

RAIN FORESTS DISCOVERIES

As the Rain Forests in the Congo continue to be clear-cut, scientists have discovered the Bononobo Apes, known as the sensitive-sexy apes, and now believed by scientists to be our closest relatives--overturning the old theories we evolved from the war-like male-dominated chimpanzees six million years ago.

Unlike other animals who have sex just to procreate, the Bononbo Apes, who have a human-like posture, have sex face-to-face for fun. Scientists have documented that sex amongst these deep rain forests apes who rarely fight, resembles the Indian Kama Sutra: not just male-female, but also same gender sex, oral sex, masturbation, and even group sex. Shame on you.

SPECIOUS CHARITIES
(Pain For Profit)

From PETA: *When you donate to a charity, do you know where the money actually goes? Could your gift be contributing to animal suffering? Some health charities ask for donations to help people with diseases and disabilities yet spend the money to bankroll horrific experiments on dogs, cats, monkeys, rabbits, rats, mice, hamsters, pigs, ferrets, frogs, fish, guinea pigs, sheep, birds, and other animals.*

While human health needs cry out for attention and so many people are going without medical care, animal experimentation enriches laboratories and scientists but drains money from relevant and effective projects that could really help save lives.

"I look at lab animals as organisms, which when injected produce medical paper-trails to prove we're working, in order to continue or obtain funding," cynical comment from a vivisector wishing to remain anonymous, regarding hir(unisex gender) views on animal research.

The **America Heart Association** funded vivisectors with your donations to severe nerves in dogs' hearts and forced chickens to breathe concentrated cigarette smoke, even though scientists have known for years that smoking causes cancer.

The America Heart Association has also funded vivisectors with your donations to cut holes in the throats of newborn lambs, slice their nerves and obstructed their breathing, despite the fact that the major advances in heart disease have been obtained from human data.

"The behavior of men to the lower animals, and their behavior to each other, bear constant relationship."

Herbert Spencer
English Philosopher

The **March of Dimes** funded vivisectors with your donations to sew the eyes of newborn kittens shut for a year, then killed them, to show that depriving cats of normal vision alters brain development--and already well known and accepted scientific fact.

The March of Dimes has also funded vivisectors with your donations to overdose pregnant animals with cocaine, nicotine, and alcohol even though the data on how these substances effects human babies is already known.

"I wish no living thing to suffer pain."

Percy Bysshe Shelley

Many of the **Red Cross'** gruesome animal experiments involve *unrelieved* pain. One experiment called for rabbits to be bled-- 22 to 30 percent of their blood volume every two weeks.

"What is the insuperable line between us and other animals? The question is not, can they reason? Can they talk? But, can they suffer?"

Jeremy Bentham
English Reformer, Philosopher & Author

Shriners Burns Institutes have conducted burn experiments on live dogs, pigs, guinea pigs, mice, and rats for years. Experimenters at Shriners reportedly burned nearly one-third of the total skin area, to test wound healing in animals treated with clenbuterolÑa drug--even though it is already used on human burn victims and with human data readily available.

172

In another experiment, Shriners Burns Institutes burned sheeps' throats to test the effect of antibiotics in fighting infection. Even though many doctors already administer antibiotics to burn victims to fight infection--so once again, there is already abundant human data available.

"No *real human being*, will wantonly murder any creature which holds its life by the same tenure that he does."

Henry David Thoreau

PETA'S HEALING WITHOUT HURTING

Instead of pillaging animals' bodies for cures to human diseases, *compassionate charities* focus their research where the *best hope* of treatment lies: with humans.

These compassionate charities realize that animal experiments are expensive, unnecessary, unreliable, and sometimes dangerously misleading. Enormous variations exist among rats, rabbits, dogs, pigs, and human beings--and meaningful scientific conclusions cannot be drawn about one species by studying another.

Non-animal methods are often less expensive and provide a more accurate method of testing and can be interpreted more objectively. Compassionate, modern charities know that we can improve treatments through up-to-date, non-animal methods. These compassionate charities also realize only non-animal research, leads to real progress in the prevention and treatment of disease--without starving, crippling, burning, poisoning, or cutting open healthy animal.

WHAT YOU CAN DO

* Before you donate to a health charity, ask if it funds animal experiments. Don't contribute until you have a written guarantee that animals are not being used.

* Let charities that fund animal tests know that you only give to those that **don't** harm animals.

* Contact PETA or other animal welfare organizations for a free list of charities that do and that **don't** fund animal experiments, **like the International Association of Firefighters Burn Foundation,** which is funding exciting alternatives to animal use, such as skin cultures, which may ultimately help not only burn victims but individuals in need of other types of tissue transplants.

"There can be nothing more pressingly necessary than for the barbarity of vivsection to be fought precisely from the scientific angle. Vivisection is not only the most cruel and loathsome, but also the worst way of conducting research, a shameful discredit to science and surest path to the brutalization of doctors and of the whole society...Every doctor who cast a stone at vivisection is performing a service to science civilization, religion and mankind."

Dr. Eduard Reich

SUCCESSFUL PRODUCTS WITHOUT PAIN

Avon Products, Inc., use to kill about 24,000 animals a year to test its products. But after an endless loop of animal welfare protests, which began affecting its sales, Avon now uses many non-animal tests, including the Eytex method in lieu of the tortuous Draize Method that scorches the eyes of restrained rabbits.

Eytex, developed by InVitro International in Irvine, Calif., assesses irritancy with a protein alteration system. A vegetable protein from the jack bean mimics the cornea's reaction when exposed to foreign matter. The greater the irritation, the more opaque the solution becomes.

174

The **Skintex formula**, also developed by InVitro International, is made from the yellowish meat of the pumpkin rind--it mimics the reaction of human skin to foreign substances. Both Eytex and Skintex can be used to determine the toxicity of more than 5,000 different materials.

In the **Neutral Red Bioassay**, a product of Clonetics Corporation in San Diego, Calif., a water-soluble dye is added to normal human skin cells in a tissue culture plate with 96 wells. A computer measures the degree to which the dye is absorbed by the cells, indicating relative toxicity and eliminating the observer bias, one of the factors that limits the effectiveness of tests on animals. EpiPack, also made by Clonetics, is the first commercial product to contain live, normal cloned human cells, which are exposed to test substances in various dilutions.

Tissue and cell cultures can be grown in the laboratory from single cells from human or animal tissues. Three companies have developed **artificial human skin** which can be used in skin grafts for burn victims and other patients and can replace animals in product tests.

Marrow-Tech, headquartered in LaJolla, Calif., makes **NeoDerm**, which begins with the injection of skin cells into a sterile plastic bag containing a biodegradable mesh. The cells attach to the mesh and grow around it, like a vine on a garden lattice. After the segment of skin is sewn onto the patient, the mesh gradually dissolves.

Biosurface Technology, of Cambridge, Mass., uses the patient's own cells to grow a skin to replace the epidermis (the top layer).

Organogenesis Inc., also of Cambridge, has found customers for its **Testskin** in Avon, Amway, Estee Lauder, and other leading cosmetics companies.

The **CAM Test** uses fertilized chicken eggs to assess eye irritancy by showing the reaction of the chorioallantoic membrane to test substances. Because this membrane has no nerve fibers, the test causes no discomfort or pain. This test is intended for use by cosmetics and household product manufacturers, but egg membranes have also been used to culture viruses and vaccines. (Although we should strive to use no animals or animal byproducts in experiments, egg membranes are preferable to sentient animals.)

VIRTUAL ORGANS have been developed by Physiome Sciences of New York. At this point they have created virtual hearts of dogs, guinea pigs, rats and mice, which simulate how drugs and other chemicals effect the real organs. These simulated organs should help drug companies select drugs that might be beneficial, and protect themselves from lawsuits.

Procter & Gamble, a perpetual animal abuser that purportedly kills thousands of animals each year for its own liability protection, and employs archaic and excruciating animal testing without sedation such as: forcing caustic chemicals into the eyes of rabbits and applying burning chemicals to the shaved and raw skin of many types of laboratory animals...And Insiders at P&G have confirmed, animals often break their necks or backs trying to reel away to escape the pain...And those animals that survive one test are then used in the next painful battery of tests....until they are finally killed...

But, P&G(known as Pain & Greed to animal welfare groups, after P&G lobbied to defeat the ban on the agonizing Draize Eye test) has understandably been the constant target of animal welfare activists, has reluctantly decided to pledge $900,000 for a supercomputer project to develop a **virtual human**. Although this is a large amount of money, it is a gesture compared to the $5.1 billion Procter & Gamble spends annually just on advertising. But, P&G has reportedly broken many promises to animal welfare groups in the past--so we'll have to wait and see.

176

BEST HOPE FOR MEDICAL APPLICATIONS

Clinical surveys, using human volunteers, case studies, autopsy reports, and statistical analyses-- permit far more accurate observation and use of actual environmental factors related to human disease than is possible with animals confined in laboratories, who contract diseases in conditions vastly different from the situations that confront humans.

Long before the famous smoking beagle experiments began, statisticians and epidemiologists knew that cigarette smoking caused *cancer in humans*, yet programs to warn people about the hazards of smoking were delayed while more animal tests were carried out to the satisfaction of the tobacco industries...Thousands of tests--blowing cigarette smoke into restrained animals for years on end...proved inconclusive to the great-glee of the tobacco companies.

Mathematical and computer models, based on physical and chemical structures and properties of a substance, can now be used to make predictions about the toxicity of a substance.

TOPKAT, a software package distributed by Health Designs Inc., predicts oral toxicity and skin and eye irritation. It "is intended to be used as a personal tool by toxicologists, pharmacologists, synthetic and medicinal chemists, regulators, and industrial hygienists, among others," according to Health Designs Inc. TOPKAT is now used by the Food and Drug Administration, the Environmental Protection Agency, and the U.S. Army.

The **Ames Test** involves mixing the test chemical with a bacterial culture of Salmonella typhimurium and adding activating enzymes to the mixture. It was able to detect 156 out of 174 (90 %) animal carcinogens and 96 out of 108 (88 %) non-carcinogens.

The **Ames Test** involves mixing the test chemical with a bacterial culture of Salmonella typhimurium and adding activating enzymes to the mixture. It was able to detect 156 out of 174 (90 %) animal carcinogens and 96 out of 108 (88 %) non-carcinogens.

The **Agarose Diffusion Method** was designed in the early 1960s to determine the toxicity of plastics and other synthetic materials used in medical devices such as heart valves, intravenous lines, and artificial joints. In this test, human cells and a small amount of test material are placed in a flask, separated by a thin layer of agarose, a derivative of the seaweed agar. If the test material is an irritant, a zone of killed cells appears around the substance.

TIME AND MONEY

Non-animal tests are generally faster and less expensive than the animal tests they replace and improve upon.

Eytex testing kits can test three concentrations of a chemical for $99.50; a cruel Draize test of comparable range would cost more than $1,000. Never mind the pain, suffering, and blinding the animals.

In cancer studies, animal tests of a single substance may take four to eight years and cost $400,000 or more, whereas short-term non-animal studies like the Ames test cost only $200-$4,000 and can be completed in one to four days.

The dangers of waiting years for results of animal tests are apparent. In 1985, the Environmental Protection Agency determined that the animal tests had not shown a sufficient degree of danger in the pesticide *Alar*, and it called on the manufacturer to conduct still more cancer studies on animals.

Now, years later, these studies are still incomplete. Although the EPA has pulled Alar from the market, non-animal tests would have taken a matter of days or months, not years, and could have meant that fewer consumers would have come into contact with hazardous Alar-treated products.

Since their inception in 1902, two-thirds of the Nobel Prizes in physiology and medicine went to projects that primarily or entirely used *alternative techniques to animal testing.*

All significant advances related to diseases such as AIDS, Alzheimer's and cancer are purported to have come from *alternative techniques to animal testing.*

"While we ourselves are the living graves of murdered animals, how can we expect any ideal conditions on this earth?"

George Bernard Shaw

FINDING ANIMAL TESTING ALTERNATIVES

NORINA, the world's largest animal alternatives database can now also be reached online. To find the current web-site address, enter "NORINA" into a search engine. NORINA holds more than 3,700 records with alternatives to vivisection and dissection. Access to this incredible database is *free*, and updated monthly.

HEALTH CHARITIES THAT TEST ON ANIMALS

To find the latest list of *health charities* that conduct or fund experiments on animals, send $3.50 to Foley Publishing, PO Box 32, Port Costa, CA 94569. All orders are shipped within 24-hours. These organizations deal with human health issues ranging from lung cancer to drug addiction to blindness.

While some of these charities do have relevant and effective projects that help improve lives, all of them drain money away from these projects into cruel experiments on animals.

They starve, cripple, burn, poison, and slice open healthy animals to study human diseases and disabilities. According to many authorities, such experiments have no practical benefit to anyone. They are unnecessary, unreliable, and sometimes dangerously misleading.

"Enormous variations exist among rats, rabbits, dogs, pigs, and human beings, and meaningful scientific conclusions cannot be drawn about one species by studying another," says Neal Barnard, M.D. "Non-animal methods provide a more accurate method of testing and can be interpreted more objectively."

Many colleges and universities have laboratories that conduct animal experiments for health and other purposes. If you would like to know if a specific school has an animal laboratory, please contact PETA. For information on the experiments being conducted and to voice your opinion, please contact the school.

Photo Obtained in 1999

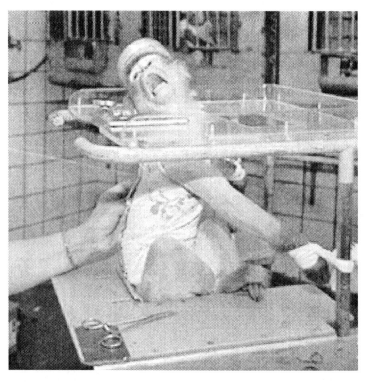

NASA's Ames Research Center

EPILOGUE

The Greatest Medical Attainments Were Achieved Without Animal Testing.

Despite billions of your tax dollars, and the countless suffering and pain still being **Intentionally** inflicted upon **Unconsenting** animals **Unnecessarily**, medical historians have repeatedly found that nothing learned from cruel animal experiments is responsible for the decline in human-animal deaths since 1900 from the most common infectious diseases, but improved nutrition, sanitation, and other behavioral and environmental factors are the main reasons we are living longer.

These facts fly in the face of the continuous medical PR bombardment released as *news* from the medical community, researchers, and other vivisectors with financial interests, and to a lesser degree medical personal carrying unresolved guilt from being part of the society-accepted vivisecting horror show.

Many of the most important advances in health are attributable to human studies, among them anesthesia; bacteriology; germ theory; the stethoscope; morphine; radium; artificial respiration; antiseptics; the CAT, MRI, and PET scans; the discovery of the relationships between cholesterol and heart disease and between smoking and cancer; the development of x-rays; and the isolation of the virus that causes AIDS. Animal testing played no role in these and many other developments.

It's time to end the barbaric cruelty of animal experiments...And stand against **Vivisection, Factory Farming**, and other **animal and human abuses** on **moral grounds**...

MORE FAMOUS VEGETARIANS:

Entertainers: Steve Martin, Brad Pitt, Brooke Shields, David Duchovny, Downtown Julie Brown, Michael J. Fox, Prince, Dustin Hoffman, Keenan Ivory Wayens, Danny De Vito, Phil Collen, Vanessa Williams, Elvis Costetllo, Daryl Hannah, Darren Hayes(Singer Savage Garden), Kim Alexis, Indigo Girls, Riki Rockett(Musician For Poison), Alec Baldwin, Des'ree, Olivia Newton John, Glady's Knight, Boy George, Billy Idol, Annie Lennox, Lenny Kravitz, Larry Hagman, Kevin Eubanks(Jay Leno Show), Pamela Anderson Lee, "Weird" Al Yankovic, Brigette Bardott, Gavin MacLeod, Michael Bolton, Woody Harrelson, Ally Sheedy, Ted Danson, Cicely Tyson, Shaun Cassidy, Lori Petty, Janeane Garofalo, Dre from Outkast(Rapper), Drew Barrymore, William Shatner, Candace Bergen, Mary Lu Henner, Casey Kasem, Jonathan Taylor Thomas, Julie Christie, David Carradine, Claudia Schiffer,Tracy Pollen, Ringo Starr, Henry Hiemlich, Kirk Cameron, Rosanna Arquette, Fred Rogers(Mr. Rogers), Joe Regalbuto, Milton Berle, Meridith Baxter, Susan St. James, Moby, Mya, Fiona Apple, Liv Tyler, Dr. Ruth(TV/Radio Sex Therapist), and Ricki Lake.

Historical: Steven Jobs(Founder Apple Computer), Thomas Edison(Inventor), Susan B. Anthony(Spearheaded Women's Suffrage Movement), Dr. Benjamin Spock(Ground Breaking Pediatrician), Andrew Jacobs(Indiana Congressman), Budda(Buddist Illuminated Sage), Louisa May Alcott(American Author and Reformer), Clara Barton(Founder American Red Cross), General William Booth(Founder Salvation Army), Ellen G. White(Founder Seventh Day Adventist Church), and Sy Sperling(Founder Hair Club for Men).

Sports Personalities: Hank Arron(Hall of Fame Baseball Player), Jack LaLanne(Fitness Guru), and Billie Jean King(American Tennis Champion).

182

S. Francis has published 100s of articles. Hir(unisex gender)first published book was a mystery. Se(unisex gender) has also optioned two screenplays.

To Order a Copy of "PAWPRINTS," Send a Check or Money Order For $13.95 to Foley Publishing Company, PO Box 32, Port Costa, CA 94569.

All Book Orders Are Shipped Within 48-Hours of Receipt. Visit Us On The World Wide Web: http://home.jps.net/kenfoley. *Pawprints* is also available online at www.amazon.com & www.barnesnoble.com and other leading booksellers.